Capital Investment Selection

An Introduction to CAPITAL INVESTMENT SELECTION

Financial Return
Strategy and Synergy
Societal Aspects

J. G. Wissema

Frances Pinter (Publishers)
London and Dover, N.H.

First published in Great Britain in 1985 by
Frances Pinter (Publishers) Limited
25 Floral Street, London WC2E 9DS

Published in the United States of America in 1985 by
Frances Pinter (Publishers), 51 Washington Street
Dover, New Hampshire

British Library Cataloguing in Publication Data

Wissema, J. G.
Capital Investment Selection.
1. Investments
I. Title
332.6 HG4521

ISBN 0-86187-491-9

Library of Congress Cataloging in Publication Data

Wissema, J. G., 1942–
Capital Investment Selection.

Translation of: Inleiding tot investeringsselectie.
Bibliography: p.
Includes index.
1. Capital investments – Evaluation. I. Title.
HG4028.C4W57713 1984 658.1'52 84-43046

Typeset by Rod-Art, Abingdon, Oxon.
Printed and bound in Great Britain by SRP Ltd., Exeter

CONTENTS

Tables

Figures

PREFACE

In capital investment selection decision-makers are confronted with the problem of what considerations tip the balance in accepting or rejecting an investment proposal. On the basis of consultancy and research activities I have come to the conclusion, during the course of the years, that there are three investment selection criteria, namely: financial return, synergy and affinity to strategy, and societal acceptability. Many companies and non-profit-making organizations sometimes use very peculiar check-lists against which the appeal of a project can be assessed, and which include a random ranking of the different aspects mentioned. In addition, financial return anaylsis is overemphasized. As Eileen M. Rudden pointed out in the *Wall Street Journal* of 1 November 1982, the problem is not with financial return techniques themselves. The problem is their frequent misapplication.

This book aims to offer an integral and systematic approach to the analysis of capital investments and other investments by companies, such as research and development projects, marketing campaigns, and reorganizations. The main objective of this book is to describe concrete methods, giving clear instructions for use, with which the appeal of the project can be checked against the given criteria. The three methods, financial return analysis, synergy/strategy profile and aspect-matrix, are explained with the help of examples. The definitions used are also described with the help of examples from commercial practice. The method of financial return analysis has existed for a long time and needs only to be moulded into a practical form; the synergy/strategy profile is completely new and links up with definitions from strategic planning. The technology assessment method has been derived from earlier papers written by me.

The main aim of this book is its practical use by managers and staff of companies as well as non-profit-making organizations; but also banks, investors and other suppliers of loans, capital or subsidies can benefit from it. For students of management science the integral investment analysis, as described in this book, should be an obligatory subject of study, since this management technique is of equal importance to reading a balance sheet or understanding cost price systems.

The book has been written in plain terms. In Chapters 2 to 4 the three methods and their backgrounds have been described. This is preceded by an introductory chapter in which the term investment is explained, and in which the thought behind the applied method of analysis is introduced. In the fifth chapter a shortened method of analysis, plus instructions for drawing up feasibility studies, is given, as well as a review of the place of the method, linking with the first chapter. A sixth chapter, with four cases describing investment selection procedures in different companies, concludes the book. A number of annexes have been added. The first two annexes give two exercises concerning a full capital investment analysis, while Annexes 3 and 4 deal with cases concerning two specific problems of financial return analysis. In all the exercises a suggested solution has been described in detail. Annexe 5 gives a method for the analysis of financial return analysis. This annexe also describes the major decisions to be made in setting up a financing scheme and contains an exercise with a detailed solution. All chapters and annexes can be read separately; the text has been attuned to non-specialists and has been kept free of difficult terms.

This book does not promise an infallible method of taking the perfect decision concerning investments: such a method can be classified, together with the perpetually burning bulb and the *perpetuum mobile*, as crying for the moon. However, use of the method will lead to a more profound understanding of what is to be expected from a capital investment and what one wants to do with it. This can lead to more and better communication; experience has shown that this itself leads to better investment decision.

As I have said before, the contents of this book are derived from commercial practice. I want to thank the managers of companies with whom I have developed and tested these methods for their contributions and co-operation. The same applies to the many participants in management seminars, fellow teachers, fellow management consultants and students, who, by their critical and often creative approach, have contributed towards the final shaping of methods and instructions. Finally, I want to thank Mrs. A.J.M. Zoet for her translation of an earlier Dutch version of this book.

I hope this book will find its way equally to managers and to students.

The Hague *J. G. Wissema*
August 1984

1. INVESTMENT AND INVESTMENT SELECTION

Why investment selection methods?

Some entrepreneurs who light on this book will tend to think: what a fuss over making a decision about whether or not to continue with an investment project. It may, therefore, be a good idea to give a short explanation at the beginning of this book as to why systematic investment selection is profitable, or, better still, why it may eventually make all the difference between the prosperity or bankruptcy of an enterprise.

Entrepreneurs are characterized by an ongoing interest in their enterprises. They participate energetically and even if they relax there is always a thought in the back of their minds as to 'What if we did this?', 'Could that problem be approached differently?', 'Is it not about time to get to know something about those new machines?', etc. These considerations are often restricted to what is called the tactical domain, the area of day-to-day business where short-term views are taken of maybe one year and sometimes only a few months.

Is this bad? Not at all: a number of enterprises would do a lot worse if this was not common practice. However, entrepreneurs do miss interesting opportunities because of this one-sided thinking. There is another way of thinking about a business which could be labelled the strategic domain. In this area more profound questions arise, such as: 'What am I really doing?', 'What is the distinction between my business and that of a competitor or another line of business?', 'What is the long-term objective of my enterprise?'

This cross-fertilization of thinking between the two domains is profitable. It can be mutally responsive and stimulating. But there is more to it than that. By being aware of what one is doing – and sharing this awareness with the rest of the staff – the enterprise will continue to head in the right direction and deviations, attractive as they may be, will be avoided. However, in doing this the enterprise should steer a middle course.

The two views should not be mutually exclusive. Considering the strategic domain alone may lead to fascinating theories, but if there is no action, they will amount to little. A lot of talk and little action is what entrepreneurs are especially afraid of. Although this fear is understandable and partly justified – a lot of strategy stories are indeed humbug – the threshold of the strategic domain of thinking is not easily reached.

Three arguments are presented to avoid this strategic domain. The first is 'Let's all work harder and we will reach our goal without all these theories'. Of course this is six of one and half a dozen of the other. A lot of enterprises have worked strenuously towards bankruptcy in this way because their competitors – and not necessarily the Japanese – did engage in new ventures. The second argument is something like 'The entrepreneurial climate is to blame for our problems and it is the government that should take care of that'. In part, a justified remark, but no reason to sit and wait. It is the entrepreneurs that have to come up to the mark in times of difficulty.

A third argument against strategic thinking is the conclusion that a lot of successful entrepreneurs never made this thinking part of their policy, nor ever will do, and yet have established leading businesses out of the blue. This can hardly be contradicted, yet it should be realized that this argument is only applicable to the pioneers who plunge into a new line of business. Each enterprise faces the moment of transition from the stage of expansion into the stage of consolidation or growth, and this requires a different approach.

The investment selection method as described in this book is a key link between the two approaches. The strategic domain leads to criteria and checkpoints for the tactical domain. Conversely, some decisions in the tactical domain will clash with these checkpoints, requiring an adjustment of the latter. Strategic thinking leads to the development of selection criteria for investment; as we shall see, three such criteria can be distinguished. The methods described in this book indicate to what extent an investment project meets these requirements. A project considered to be as strong as iron may yet not come up to the requirements. This may be caused by too optimistic an analysis of the project, but also by a different way of thinking, to which the requirements should be adjusted. This dual tactical and strategic approach gives an excellent insight, resulting in better decisions.

Investment selection methods like the ones described in this book are no guarantee of perfect decisions that will automatically lead to prosperity and growth of the organization. This would be just as impossible as the perpetual motion. The real advantages that result from the use of these methods can be summarized as follows:

(i) Using the methods calls for the expression of the investment requirements in words. This leads to a two-sided approach to the investment and other business matters within the organization – the tactical and strategic approach. This dual approach yields a more penetrating insight into the business and the question of whether the investment is synergistic or not.

(ii) The appeal of an investment cannot be exactly assessed. However, we dare say that the methods described in this book identify both the very good and the very bad projects.

(iii) The methods give an insight into susceptibility to technical and commercial changes. Suppose the appeal of a certain investment project is analysed with the help of the methods in this book, if the project undergoes a slight change, it is possible to ascertain reasonably exactly whether these changes render the project more or less appealing.

(iv) Moreover, the use of the methods has a considerable communicative power. People from different areas such as marketing/sales, production, and often research and development and financing, have to gather round the table to make an analysis and they will be confronted with various views and requirements; this is of the utmost importance. When discussing the project with a group in the language of methods people will find out both the pros and cons of the project and its final objective.

(v) Finally, investment selection methods provide a compact common language of communication with financiers, supervisors, shareholders and others who play a part in the decision-making.

Analytical investment selection will therefore be a must for each enterprise, big or small, expansive or consolidating, and every other organization investing in fixed assets, know-how or services.

What are investments?

Expenses within an enterprise or other organization may be divided into investments and – what we will call in this book – operating costs. An investment is: spending money on assets having a long life, i.e. something that is to the best advantage of the enterprise for more than one year. This may be land, buildings and machinery – called fixed assets – but in some instances also know-how, reputation, goodwill, etc. Operating costs are spent on one-off purchases, such as raw materials, wages and energy supply.

Therefore, investment decisions differ from other financial decisions in that the commodity obtained or purchased can be used again. This requires long-term planning. Consequently, in view of the relatively large amounts that investments require, investment decisions call for a different approach to decisions about operating costs. Investments and operating costs also require different pay-back periods for the expenses. Operating costs will have to be matched by the income in the same year that they are incurred; otherwise, apart from special circumstances, the enterprise incurs a loss. The pay-back period for investments, however, is not limited to the same year. Their use extends over more than one year so, obviously, the expenses may also be spread over more than one year; the investment, therefore, pays back little by little over the years. In bookkeeping terms the investment is depreciated in more than one year. This means that in calculating profit or loss – in principle done by deducting the operating costs from the gross sales – the entire amount invested is not deducted from the gross sales, but a certain percentage, for example, 10 or 20 per cent, for a number of years. Consequently, that part of the investment not yet depreciated should be presented on the asset side of the balance, since it represents a certain value.

This spreading of the investment expenses over more than one year is called converting or transforming into assets, literally: enter on the asset side of the balance sheet. One may say that investment expenses are converted into assets and operating costs are not. On the profit and loss account the total amount of operating costs is presented, but only the depreciations of the investments are shown and when the entire investment has been depreciated, nothing is shown.

Crucial to every investment are these questions:

What are the costs?
What is the return?
Can the internal and external side-effects be anticipated?

In asking these questions, the verb 'to invest' should be viewed more broadly than just investment in land, buildings, machinery and working capital, which will be compensated for by selling products or services. This broadening is required as the return may be immaterial in kind. In some instances the value may be assessed as in, for example, investment in procedures or the structure of an organization. But if the objective of the investment is goodwill or reputation such an analysis is hardly feasible. Consequently, the imponderables have generally been neglected, which leads to the use of an investment definition to the following effect:

Investing is tying up capital in order to obtain, in an active way, a durable flow of income.

According to this (narrow) definition, laying out a park by a local authority would not be an investment because it only requires more money. Yet a park and road safety facilities do contribute to the immaterial 'income' of those who use them. Within an enterprise there are also many examples on investments that do not yield income in terms of money, but which are aimed at improving working conditions.

A second adjustment to the definition is required because of its side-effects. No enterprise will welcome investment in a factory which causes serious environmental pollution, even if the law will permit it and the returns can be paid. Thus, other 'soft' external constraints should be mentioned.

However, there are also internal constraints, closely connected to the long-term objectives of the organization. Consequently, financial return is not the only criterion for the approval of the projects. This leads to a second, more general definition:

Investing is tying up capital or making money available within the limits of external and internal constraints, in order to obtain a long-lasting advantage in an active way.

The answers to the questions 'What are the cost' and 'What is the return' will be given by applying the financial return analysis techniques if the investments and the proceeds can be expressed in terms of money. The demand that the proceeds should be in excess of the expense can be called the first criterion, or the financial return criterion.

However, decisions are not made by financial return only. Projects close to present activities, following up a lead or advantage and avoiding disadvantages which outweigh them, are to be preferred. The demand that the investment should link with the existing strong/weak points of the enterprise is called the second criterion or synergistic/strategic criterion.

For lack of a better name we call the third criterion the integral societal acceptability criterion. In this criterion possible side-effects are analysed in as broad a sense as possible. This is done by technology assessment.

Investments not transformed into assets

Although it may have been suggested it is not always possible to make a clear distinction on whether or not to transform expenses into assets. Some expenses have the nature of an investment, because they involve a long-term tying up of money or manpower, the results of which can also be used repeatedly. Yet they are not converted into assets. An example of this are the research and development costs (R&D). These expenses yield a certain amount of know-how which may be of use in different places or projects. Know-how, as with buildings and machinery, constitutes a long-lasting asset for an enterprise; all these tie up the activities of the enterprise for a longer period of time.

Most R&D projects, therefore, have the typical nature of an investment, yet in general they are not converted into assets, and consequently they are not spread over more than one year. There are three reasons for this.

First, a positive decision on an R&D project does not necessarily mean that it will yield know-how to the advantage of the enterprise; there is a certain amount of uncertainty. If this know-how is put on the asset side of the balance sheet the resulting picture may be too bright: both the invested capital (this is the balance sheet value) and the equity have been overvalued if the know-how should later prove to have little value in practice. A careful entrepreneur rather writes off R&D costs instantly as part of what is called 'good business practice'.

The second reason for not putting R&D costs on the asset side of the balance sheet is the fiscal advantage it yields. For the enterprise's profit is subjected to corporation tax and, in principle, profit equals income minus expenses and depreciation. When certain costs are deducted from the income in one go, the profit will be smaller in that year and less tax will have to be paid than when only 10 per cent, for example, is deducted as depreciation. The remaining 90 per cent will be deducted in the following years, of course, yielding fiscal advantages then. So the decision on whether or not to convert into assets does not affect the entire tax deduction. However, not converting only brings the advantage of tax deduction sooner, which is almost always attractive.

Finally, the third reason for not transforming R&D costs into assets lies in the fact that know-how, goodwill, etc. are in general not accepted by banks as security for loans. This fact as such is not sufficient reason for not putting the R&D costs on the asset side of the balance sheet, but it certainly limits the possibilities. This does lead to a distortion of the value of investments in the service sector as compared to those in industrial enterprises and to bigger problems for service industries to secure loans for investment from banks. In principle, a bank only loans money against a tangible security.

We hope to have made clear that R&D costs should be considered to be and treated as investments but that they should not be transformed into assets. The same applies to depth-investments in the market, major reorganization costs and corporate advertising – three matters that should be considered to be and treated as investments – but which will not be put on the asset side of the balance sheet in view of the risks they entail, the fiscal advantage they yield and their non-tangible nature.

Intuitive versus rational approach

An entrepreneur or a manager of a non-profit-making organization will consider an investment proposal basically in two ways. On the one hand he or she will intuitively consider the appeal of the proposal. He will not give the go-ahead to an investment that has no intuitive appeal, even if the outlook on paper is excellent. On the other hand he will sometimes push something through which has immense intuitive appeal, even if analysis proves that the chances for success are poor.

Apart from this intuitive approach there is the analytical approach, a rational systematic analysis of the likelihood of success of the investment. Sometimes management scientists are of the opinion that this is the only way and that only old-fashioned entrepreneurs take decisions based on intuitive considerations. It was Mintzberg[1] who showed us that we have to be careful in airing such an opinion and that both approaches supplement each other. The author of this book, who sometimes compares an entrepreneur to an artist, agrees with this view and notes that it is the interaction between the two approaches that yields profitable results. According to Freud the rational domain should have good access to the intuitive domain, otherwise neuroses are likely to develop. Anyone having to make an important personal choice uses both approaches, for example when choosing a partner, friends, study, job, house, etc.

This book deals only with the analytical approach. As has been explained, three criteria can be distinguished for an investor to come to a decision. Each criterion will subsequently lead to the development of an analytical technique.

Criteria for investment selection

The first and oldest criterion is that of financial return – the expected financial return on the capital invested. Investments should sooner or later bring in more money than the expenses associated with them, preferably sooner, but in some cases later will be equally good. A new machine will only be bought if it yields more economical advantages than the money spent on purchase, maintenance and consumption of energy. A new business activity will only be started when the anticipated return will amply cover the investment and initial expenses.

However, companies do not decide on the basis of financial return alone. An example will clarify this. A textile company, established in a Southern European country, had prospered for many years. The management had been able to consolidate a large share of the market, by means of good technology and import protection. In the main the profits had been used to finance the growth of the company. When the market growth in that country came to a halt there were no further opportunities for expansion and other investment proposals had to be considered. Export was out of the question, production being too expensive because of its small-scale structure. They decided to diversify, i.e. develop new business activities over and above the existing activities. A group of energetic young managers was set up, and they came forward with an interesting project in as little as a month's time. The project consisted of a transport undertaking with a hundred tipping cars used in road construction. The financial return criterion was met: a number of orders were included in the take-over of the company, which would realize a pay-back period of the investment of less than two years. The long-term outlook was excellent: there were hardly any good roads in the country and the government had clear-cut plans for the improvement of the infrastructure. The reasons why the company was on offer did not arouse any suspicion and the risk was limited because the take-over investment was only a small part of the invested capital of the mother company.

Should one accept or reject such an investment proposal? The answer is: it depends on one's course of action after the take-over. Do you consider the take-over to be an opportunity, a windfall? Then the risks are great. Making the daughter company profitable will entail canvassing of orders, which will require, apart from a considerable amount of technical know-how, contacts with the government and local authorities. Is not this alien to a textile company? The chances that the company will fail completely after an initial success are considerable.

Yet the take-over can be very appealing. Suppose the company, after having realized that diversification is essential, deliberately chooses to set up a road construction division, which is big enough to function as the 'second leg' of the company, apart from its textile activities. In that case management and expertise will be recruited and the take-over of the transport company may fit in excellently with this strategy.

Thus, apart from the financial return criterion, laying down the requirements for the financial return on the capital invested, there is a strategic investment criterion that states that the investment should fit in with the strategy of the enterprise; in the example the strategy was diversification. In order to assess whether an investment proposal comes up to this requirement the affinity to strategy should be assessed.

Synergy

Apart from these strategic considerations there are synergistic considerations. Synergy is the advantage which emerges from a combination of activities, for example a car-pool for commuter traffic, or a sausage manufacturer who merges with a manufacturer of ready-fried chips, so that they can both use one instead of two delivery vans.

Suppose two companies, *A* and *B*, independently decide to develop a new product. And suppose *A* has extensive experience with this kind of product and *B* has not. Then the chances that *A* will present a good project in time are better than those of *B*. We then say that this project has more 'synergy' with company *A* than with company *B*. The reader will understand where this leads to: on the one hand, in choosing investment projects, synergy is an important criterion: the higher the synergy the more the likelihood of success. On the other hand, projects with little synergy may sometimes be preferred when a company wants to diversify and strategic considerations are the touchstone.

A fictitious example: suppose a company expects a ready market for a certain new product and for that reason decides to develop a number of activities to that end, such as development activities, setting up a sales organization, production units and doing market research. Suppose this leads to a proposal for developing a certain product with a number of qualities that will find a ready market. Such a project will score high in the strategy but is not likely to have much synergy with existing activities.

The term synergy requires some refining before it fits in with the objective of this book. The borderline between synergy and financial return is not always as clear as it seems. For in case monetary advantages emerge from the combination of activities these advantages are included in the financial return analysis. Only non-monetary or speculative advantages will be included in the synergy analysis, otherwise the effects will be counted twice.

This can be clarified by an example. A company made an investment analysis for a project that could be built on their existing site. This yielded great financial advantages. Power, for example, could be supplied from existing generators so that new ones did not have to be bought. The costs of maintenance service were low and those for gatemen almost non-existent since existing facilities could be used. Only marginal costs, however, are included in the financial return analysis; those facilities that already exist will not have to be paid for another time. Later, in budgeting, the costs will be spread pro rata over the various projects occupying the site. This is a synergistic advantage, but since it can be expressed in monetary terms, it will be included in the financial return analysis and not in the synergy analysis.

It will be different if the technical staff says: we would like to have that new project because we can learn a lot from it to the benefit of our work in the old plant. In such a case the advantages cannot be expressed in monetary terms, they are clearly speculative and should therefore be included in the synergy analysis.

Sometimes the strategic requirements and the synergistic requirements are contradictory in a new project, but this is not always so. When the strategy is 'remain strong in current products', strategic and synergistic requirements will work in the same direction. Generally speaking, in offensive strategies the requirements are contradictory and in consolidating strategies they work in the same direction.

Societal aspects

There is a third criterion. Suppose a certain project yields sufficient financial return, is synergistic to the company, but shows environmental or safety aspects which arouse much opposition among employees and the public. Or suppose a project requires scarce raw materials, or a labour force that is hard to obtain. One should be aware of these aspects beforehand in order to avoid, after the project has been realized, being confronted with the need for new action and/or the necessity for drastic reconsideration. When a real danger has been overlooked, it can have far-reaching consequences, in view of current technology. This has both an ethical and an economic side. One does not want to act irresponsibly, even if those actions are not in conflict with the law from a formal point of view because there are not (as yet) laws against them. On the other hand, readjusting an investment project once it has already been realized may be very expensive and can lead to maximum delay and negative publicity, which may be equally expensive.

So the third criterion, according to which a decision is being made whether or not to take an investment project in hand, is the integral societal acceptability criterion. A project should be beneficial to the company, but also to society. When the latter is not the case the company will sooner or later queer its own pitch. The reader may think that his company has no major environmental or safety problems. He should, however, realize that the introduction of a number of new products can entail far-reaching consequences for society. This is not a priori a reason to stop investing, but one should be well aware of these consequences and resulting public opposition due to the environmental, scarcity and safety aspects. The societal acceptability can be assessed and optimized by means of techniques called 'technology assessment'.[2]

Investment risks

In the investment selection methods to be described three criteria are used to assess the appeal of an investment in the best possible way. When the project is actually executed it will appear more often than not that the reality is quite different from the original analysis. The entrepreneur knows beforehand that investing entails risks. As there are three investment criteria, there are in principle also three types of investment risks, which should be clearly distinguished.

In the financial return criterion two types of risk can be distinguished, i.e. the development risk and the commercial risk. Development risk includes all activities taking place before production and sales can be effected. Examples of this risk are: the R&D activities take longer or are more expensive than anticipated, the developed product appears to be of an inferior quality or higher cost, installing the machines takes longer than anticipated, and so on. The commercial risk is run when production and sales are started: are the sales prices lower and are the goods less marketable than anticipated? If so, the profits will be lower.

These two are the most recognizable elements of the entrepreneurial risk. Besides, there are the strategic, synergistic and societal risks which arise when results do not come up to expectations. These types of entrepreneurial risk are much more dangerous than those involved in the development of commercial risks. Societal acceptance may be a matter of success or failure, whereas the absence of a follow-up of strategic growth investment may lead to the 'giant among dwarfs' company type (one major activity with lots of small side-lines), which has to be trimmed off and slimmed down afterwards at great trouble and expense.

The various types of investment risk will be dealt with, wherever necessary, in the chapters to come and they have been mentioned here to indicate the structure of the book at the outset.

Summary

Investment decisions have to be distinguished from decisions about operating costs. This means the use of criteria other than those of, for example, the purchasing department. In principle, investments are put on the asset side of the balance sheet, but there are expenses which have the nature of investments which are not converted into assets.

There are two approaches to the question of whether an investment proposal should be accepted or rejected: the rational and the intuitive approach. These approaches are complementary and should be used side by side. There are three investment selection criteria:

financial return
synergy and strategy
societal acceptance

In the chapters to come methods will be described for each of these aspects by which an analysis of the project's appeal can be made.

The entrepreneurial risk means that there is a possibility that the real results of an investment may be lower than anticipated in the analysis. This leads to five types of entrepreneurial risk, i.e:

the development risk
the commercial risk
the strategic risk
the synergy risk
the societal risk.

2. FINANCIAL RETURN

Introduction

When people have a sum of money at their disposal and have no immediate use for it they can bank it at interest. In this case the money yields a certain amount of interest and, after the agreed period has expired, the principal sum will be paid back.

It is also possible to invest the money in other ways, such as shares, or participation in a company entitling the owner to a share in the profits. One cannot make sure beforehand whether the company will make a profit or, if it does, whether a dividend will be paid out. Moreover, if one wants to withdraw the money, it is not the amount originally invested that will be paid back, but the market value of the shares on the day of selling.

Within an enterprise, if it is sound, opportunities for investment are continually emerging. At the same time means will continually become available within the enterprise – again, if it is sound – which can be used for long-term investment. An entrepreneur will invest these amounts in the best possible way. Irrespective of his other considerations, he hopes to get a better financial return than when he banks the money. On the other hand, this anticipated higher financial return is marked by an uncertainty. He does not know what the value of his investment will be after a certain time. Moreover, he takes a risk. He analyses the costs and returns of various investments and has to wait and see whether his analysis proves right. Just as with the investor, the entrepreneur has no way of knowing what financial return his investment will yield and how much it will be worth after a certain time. But, unlike most shareholders, the entrepreneur has a lot of know-how concerning his investments and on the basis of that he can make an analysis of the financial return of his investment. Those kinds of analyses are called financial return analyses. Because these analyses require calculations they are also called financial return calculations. However, since this term suggests a figure that can be exactly established, which is not the case, we prefer the term financial return analysis or estimation of financial return.

In this chapter we will first explain the methods of calculation. If he wishes to do so, the reader can skip this part and turn directly to the description of the method (see p. 31).

Two principles for assessing the financial return

In principle there are two ways of assessing the financial return of an investment:

(a) assessing the pay-back period of the original investment;
(b) assessing how much money the project yields within a certain period of time (e.g. ten years) and comparing this amount with the original investment.

An example: suppose in year 1 an amount $1,000 is invested and gross sales and costs in years 2 to 10 subsequently equal (Table 2.1). In order to make the calculation the costs are deducted from the gross sales. The difference is the income and these amounts should justify the investment of $1,000. To assess the project's appeal we calculate the accumulated income by adding the income over a certain year to that of all preceding years. Then we see that:

(a) the pay-back period of the investment was achieved in the course of the fourth year, to be precise in 3.4 years or three years and five months. For, after three years $800 is paid back and 0.4 of the income of year 4 totalling $500 is $200 which makes $1,000.
(b) the return over the first ten years is estimated at

$4,200 not including the possible scrap value of the investment. In view of the investment of $1,000, the result is not bad.

All in all the investment seems to have an appeal, but a few simplifications have been applied, which have affected the result. These simplifications will be corrected in due course.

Table 2.1 Simplified calculation

Year	Gross sales (*a*)	Costs (*b*)	Income ($c = a - b$)	Accumulated income ($C = \Sigma c$)
2	1,500	1,200	300	300
3	2,000	1,500	500	800
4	2,100	1,600	500	1,300
5	2,300	1,700	600	1,900
6	2,400	1,800	600	2,500
7	2,500	2,000	500	3,000
8	2,700	2,200	500	3,500
9	2,800	2,400	400	3,900
10	2,800	2,500	300	4,200

Note: In this and following schemes the quantities are indicated by the same symbols. Capital symbols stand for accumulated quantities.

Tax and depreciation

The first simplification that is to be corrected is the fact that the company's earnings are subject to corporation tax. This tax is assumed to be 50 per cent in our examples. It is charged on the amounts from the column 'income', however, after the investment costs have been charged against the income, as the investment costs and the amounts in the current cost column may be deducted from the taxable income.

This deduction may be effected in two ways. By far the most investments are being turned into assets (compare Table 2.2), which means that the investment expenses are spread over the results of more than one year. In our example we could spread the $1,000 over the results of the first five years. These amounts are called depreciations: the investment is said to be depreciated in five years. In bookkeeping this is done in the following way (for convenience sake we leave out the proceeds and costs columns from the previous table).

Table 2.2 Calculation including taxation

Year	Invest -ment	Income	Deprecia -tion	Income before tax	Tax	ROI- in- come	Cash flow	Accumulated cash flow
	q	$a-b$	d = 20% of q	$e = a-b-d$	f = 50% of e	$g = e-f$	$s = g+d-q$	$S = \Sigma s$
1	1,000						(1,000)	(1,000)
2		300	200	100	50	50	250	(750)
3		500	200	300	150	150	350	(400)
4		500	200	300	150	150	350	(50)
5		600	200	400	200	200	400	350
6		600	200	400	200	200	400	750
7		500		500	250	250	250	1,000
8		500		500	250	250	250	1,250
9		400		400	200	200	200	1,450
10		300		300	150	150	150	1,600

Note: Negative amounts are in parentheses.

A tax of 50 per cent is imposed upon the difference between income (c) and depreciation (d). This yields (e), the pre-tax income. When we deduct the tax we get the so-called ROI-income (g), which consequently equals the gross sales (a), minus costs (b), minus depreciations (d), minus tax (f). So $g = a-b-d-f$. However, this is an arithmetical amount. The real cash flow (the income, after tax has been deducted) equals the ROI-income plus depreciations. Cash flow represents the money actually spent or left over. The first year $1,000 is spent. In the second year $1,500 ($a$) is received and $1,200 costs ($b$) and $50 tax ($f$) is being paid. Hence the cash flow (s) is $250.

In this way the cash flows for each subsequent year can be calculated and from that the accumulated cash flow (S).

From this last column we can conclude that:

(a) the pay-back period of the project was 4.125 years;
(b) the project's total proceeds equal $1,600, plus any possible proceeds after year 10.

The investment of $1,000 yields $2,600 after taxation; if the project continues the company's proceeds will amount to $1,600.

The above-mentioned case is presented on the assumption that the enterprise will make a profit each year. If a loss is incurred no tax will be levied because the profits of this project will be settled with the losses of the other activities of the enterprise. In making investment decisions these circumstances are not taken into consideration. What we want to know is whether the project is economically sound and any possible extra income resulting from the fact that existing losses can be recouped should be left out of the decision-making. Whether measures to stimulate investment, for example tax exemption for a number of years, accelerated depreciation of capital allowances, are taken into account depends upon the financial policy of the enterprise. The same applies to investment grants. In our examples we do not allow for these advantages (conservative financial policy).

The development risks

Although research costs tie up the capital of the enterprise for a longer period of time and consequently can be regarded as investment expenses, it would not be wise to consider research costs as assets (compare pp. 6–8). For whether past research will indeed yield financial return remains to be seen and it is almost inconceivable for another enterprise to take over the partly acquired know-how at cost.

Good business practice requires a careful consideration of assets, thus putting only those items on the balance sheet that are worth the amount for which they are presented. As a rule, research costs cannot be considered as such and are therefore written off as operational costs (category (b) in our example). Besides, this has the added advantage of making them directly tax-deductible as costs.

Sometimes research projects are indeed converted into assets, namely development projects with an expected success rate of almost 100 per cent. Whether items are converted into assets or not is highly dependent on the financial policy of the enterprise and the attitude of controller and accountant. Consequently, if we want to construct a calculation method it should contain both possibilities of whether or not research costs are converted into assets. However, as a rule there is no convertion into assets by way of precaution.

Apart from this precaution, the risks of research projects can be charged in another way. The thought behind this requires clarification: it comes down to the fact that we expect a financial return on research as a whole. This means that the sound research projects have to pay for the bad ones. Next, this thesis has to be translated into bookkeeping terms. We do so by including fictional costs in the calculation instead of the actual research costs, in such a way that:

$$\text{fictional costs} = \frac{\text{actual costs}}{\text{likelihood of success}}$$

Suppose we spend \$1,000 on a research project in year 1 and \$2,000 in year 2. What are the chances that we achieve our objective in year 1? Suppose this is estimated at 50 per cent or 0.5. In this case we include \$1,000 divided by 0.5 = \$2,000 as fictional costs. If the project is not discontinued after year 1 it means that the likelihood of success will be higher in year 2. If we estimate this likelihood at 80 per cent, the fictional research costs will be \$2,000 divided by 0.8 = \$2,500.

The initial percentage of the likelihood of success will gradually increase up to 100 per cent when the project is completed. The percentages will have to be assessed by a multi-disciplinary team of experts (research, marketing, production) for each year the project is in research.

Many other ways exist to analyse research projects,[3] but

these are often theoretical in kind. Before we add this risk-correction to the calculation scheme we have to apply another correction.

Discounting

In Table 2.2 all amounts have been accumulated under S as if they were of the same value. However, this is not the case, since the value of a dollar today is greater than that of a dollar say in about five years' time. The difference is the interest. Suppose we bank a dollar at an interest of 10 per cent; the value of this dollar after five years of compound interest will be \$1.61, i.e. $\$1 \times (1.10)^5$; This means that today's dollar is of the same value as \$1.61 in five years, assuming an interest of 10 per cent is feasible. Conversely, the value of a dollar received in five years will be, today, $\$1 \times (1.10)^{-5} = \$0.62$. Should the rate of interest be 10 per cent, all amounts for year 5 would have to be divided by 1.61 in order to make them comparable to the amounts that have to be spent now. This is called discounting. The 10 per cent represents the discount rate. Discounting the cash flows in the table leads to discounted cash flows, generally indicated by DCF. We can also say that future amounts are converted into present value and that the present value of \$1.61 in year 5 equals \$1. With a view to bookkeeping, discounting or converting into present value is done as in Table 2.3, allowing for a discount rate of 10 per cent.
If we apply the discount correction:

(a) The pay-back period will be 4.8 years. This is also called the Discounted Pay Back Period (DPBP); the term pay-back period itself is mostly applied to the pay-back period without applying discounting, just as in our previous example.
(b) The value of the project will be \$663 (today's dollars). This is called net present value (NPV) of the project after, in this case, ten years.

Observe that the net present value is equivalent to the accumulated discounted cash flow.

Table 2.3 Discounting

Year i	Cash flow s	Discounting factor* t	DCF $u = s/t$	Accumulated DCF $U = \Sigma u$
1	(1,000)	1.10	(909)	(909)
2	250	1.21	207	(702)
3	350	1.33	263	(439)
4	350	1.46	240	(199)
5	400	1.61	248	49
6	400	1.77	226	275
7	250	1.95	128	403
8	250	2.14	117	520
9	200	2.36	85	605
10	150	2.59	58	663

* The discounting factor equals 1.10^i, assuming a discount rate of 10 per cent per year. It is assumed that discounting starts immediately in the first year.

In the preceding calculations the possible remaining value or scrap value of the project has not been taken into account. This scrap value should always be kept low in order to avoid too optimistic a picture. A good rule of thumb is the following:

scrap value = 80 per cent of the working capital (see below)
plus 60 per cent of the original cost of the land
plus 20 per cent of the original cost of buildings and machinery

When we proceed with our calculations we shall not take the scrap value into account. (N.B. The scrap value may also be highly negative if the social cost of closing down an enterprise is included such as the case of the closing down costs of a nuclear power plant, for example.)

The working capital is the stock of money consisting of

liquid or semi-liquid resources such as bank balances, cash, debtors and stocks. An entry for the working capital and expansion of the working capital will be included in the calculations.

The corrections so far dealt with, such as payment of tax, converting into assets, development risks and discounting, turn Table 2.2 into the 'Financial return analysis form' (Table 2.7), which can at this point be checked by the reader up to line U, inclusive.

Criteria for financial return

The first criterion for financial return we have encountered is the pay-back period or the discounted pay-back period. Subsequently, we came across the method on net present value, a method in which discounting is continually applied. The advantage of the pay-back method is its simplicity, but the disadvantage is that fast-scoring and probably equally fast drying-up projects are preferred over slower starting projects which will, however, provide a long-term contribution to the cash flow. For, whatever happens after the pay-back period is not taken into consideration.

In the NPV (and for that matter also in the DPBP) the question is what discount rate is to be used. In general the interest on bank loans is taken; when the NPV turns out to be negative it is more advisable to bank the money. Naturally, when comparing projects, the percentage should be the same for each project. Furthermore, when using the NPV method one has to choose the period that has to be taken into consideration. In our example we have chosen a period of ten years, which is common practice in organizations which have, as a rule, a short development period (up to, say, four years). In case the research and development period is longer (with seed-sowing improvements, for example, it may run to ten years) or in case of a long-term investment (blast furnaces, for example) a longer period should be chosen. It is also conceivable that an entrepreneur deliberately decides in favour of a very short period of, say, five years.

The shorter the (discounted) pay-back period or the higher the NPV per invested dollar the more appealing the project.

The latter yields the fraction:

$$\frac{\text{net present value}}{\text{investment}}$$

and the higher the outcome, the more appealing the project.

A way to bypass the choice of the discount rate is the internal rate of return method. This method lies between the DPBP and NPV methods. In the DPBP the pay-back period is the moment at which the accumulated discounted cash flow is becoming positive (column Accumulated DCF in Table 2.3). When a higher discount rate is calculated the positive amounts of later years weigh less heavy and the discounted pay-back period will increase and the NPV decrease. This calculation with a higher discount rate can be repeated until the pay-back period equals the number of years used in calculating the NPV (in our example ten years); the NPV is then equal to zero.

The discount rate yielding this result is called the internal rate of return. Thus the IRR is the percentage at which the NPV, taken over a period of, say, ten years, is exactly equal to zero. With the help of our example we can clarify this graphically in Figure 2.1. In this diagram both the net present value (NPV) as a function of the discount rate, and the discounted pay-back period (DPBP) also as a function of this percentage, are represented. Two check points have already been calculated. For a percentage equal to zero it appears from Table 2.2 that NPV = $1,600 and DPBP = 4.1 years. From Table 2.3 it appeared that at 10 per cent the NPV = $663 and the DPBP = 4.8 years. In Table 2.4, the NPV and DPBP have been calculated at discount rates between 0 and 30 per cent and subsequently itemized in Figure 2.1. From Table 2.4 and Figure 2.1 it appears that the NPV is gradually decreasing and the DPBP is gradually increasing. At a percentage of 27.5 per cent the NPV = 0 and the DPBP = 10 years. In this example the internal rate of return is therefore 27.5 per cent and from a financial point of view the project has a high appeal.

From the example it appears that it is impossible to make a simple IRR calculation with the help of a formula. It will be necessary to apply various percentages until the net present values just above and just below zero have been found, and subsequently the IRR can be found by interpolation. Enterprises which regularly make financial return analyses usually have a computer program to do this trial-and-error work automatically. Such a program can be written in a few hours.

Table 2.4 Internal rate of return

Discount rate	Net present value (NPV)	Discounted pay-back period
0	$1,600	4.1 year
2	1,353	4.2
4	1,137	4.4
6	959	4.5
8	799	4.6
10	663	4.8
12	544	5.0
14	438	5.2
16	345	5.4
18	267	5.7
20	198	5.9
22	134	6.5
24	80	7.2
26	32	8.3
28	(10)	>10
30	(18)	>10

Once such a program is available it is fairly easy to calculate what Mulder has called the 'equivalence curve'.[4] In this curve the IRR is calculated with varying periods for the investment. Such a curve presents an excellent insight into the financial return development of an investment because it also clarifies the development after the standard term of, say, ten years. However, the equivalence curve will not be dealt with in this book and we refer connoisseurs to the paper mentioned. To the IRR method applies: the higher the internal rate of return, the more appealing the project. Generally, the selection criterion of an enterprise is the demand for at least some minimal IRR; this is called cut-off rate. If the IRR is higher than the cut-off rate the financial return will be sufficient; otherwise it is not.

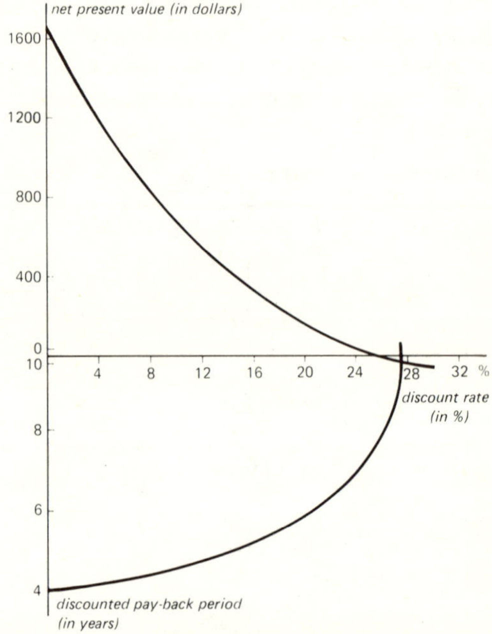

Figure 2.1 Net present value and discounted pay-back period as functions of the discount rate

How high should the cut-off rate be? The project should yield a better rate of return than the net interest. In principle this means bank interest minus inflation minus bank commission – the real reward earned by the lender for allowing the borrower to use his money. Subsequently, inflation needs to be compensated for, because our starting point has been that inflation has been taken into account in all analyses of returns and costs. There is also the entrepreneurial risk that has to be compensated for by a higher rate of return than could be obtained from investments that bear no risk. Finally, an allowance has to be made for the general overhead cost; this will also be reflected in an extra charge on the cut-off rate. To summarize:

cut-off rate = net interest
plus inflation percentage
plus extra charge entrepreneurial risk
plus extra charge general overhead costs

Most enterprises have a cut-off rate of 12 to 14 per cent; ten years ago this percentage was 18 to 20 per cent. If the calculation is made without allowing for inflation it will be obvious that the inflation component should be left out. Approaches with and without inflation may lead to different conclusions.[5]

The correlation between the three methods has been expressed in Table 2.5. In the pay-back method the period has to be calculated in which the net present value is equal to zero at a given discount rate (which can also be equal to zero when there is no discounting). In the NPV method the period is given (e.g. ten years) and the net present value is to be calculated at a given discount rate. Finally, with the internal rate of return method the discount rate rendering the net present value equal to zero is to be found for a given period.

Table 2.5 Correlation between the methods

	Time frame	Net present value	Discount rate
Pay-back method	To be computed	Zero	Given, or zero
IRR method	Given, e.g. 10 years	Zero	To be computed
NPV method	Given, e.g. 10 years	To be computed	Given

Which method to choose?

Which method is to be preferred in practice? According to most authors the net present value is by far to be preferred to the pay-back and internal rate of return methods, both having only very limited usefulness.[6] As has been noted before, the pay-back method leaves all cash flows after the pay-back period out of consideration. To take an example – the acquisition of an oilfield with large reserves but limited winning capacity and a long start-up period – this project will be a bad option when using the pay-back method, whereas it may be an excellent investment. On the other hand, a project yielding a high financial return in, for example, the first two years but which runs dry after that scores high in the pay-back method. Although the method is not very indicative, there is still a desire to have the pay-back period calculated. In case a loan has to be secured for the project it may be worth knowing whether the project can redeem the loan in the short term. Moreover, the advantage of the pay-back method is the simplicity of its calculation (the more so if discounting does not take place) and the simplicity of its interpretation; data such as present value and internal rate of return remain rather abstract notions, hard to interpret for those who are not familiar with them.

The disadvantage of the internal rate of return method with respect to the net present value method is that the former does not indicate how much money the investment requires. If there is an option between two projects this may be the decisive factor. Apart from that, when comparing two investment projects the IRR method may simply lead to mistakes. In Franks and Scholefield[7] an example is given of two projects requiring an investment of $15,000 and $10,000 respectively, with an IRR of 20 per cent and 18 per cent respectively. When using the IRR method the first project would consequently be preferred. However, if the IRR of the additional investment of $5,000 is calculated it appears to be a mere 14 per cent. At a cut-off rate of, say, 16 per cent this $5,000 can be invested in a third project with an IRR greater than this 16 per cent and the second project becomes the better option. In this introductory book all the details will not be covered, but suffice it to say that the NPV method is by far the safest method. However, the argument may be put forward that the IRR is a concept with a greater appeal than the NPV because of its simplicity.

To summarize: if a quick indication is desired primarily of the short-term effects of the investment, then use the pay-back method, without discounting. However, anyone who wants to have a clear picture should calculate all three data with discounting and eventually put his trust in the net present value.

A special problem arises if a project requires more money

than anticipated, and/or exceeds the planning time, resulting in a later inflow of income than expected. It is then necessary to draw up a further financial return analysis and the question arises as to whether (research) costs already incurred should be included in the calculation or not. It can be argued that this is unnecessary, for the costs incurred have already been spent and in taking an investment decision one should weigh the means (yet) to be spent against the (extra) income. Moreover, when the costs already incurred are included there is every chance of the project losing its appeal.[8]

On the other hand, the discipline needed to assess the financial return in the best possible way is seriously undermined if extra resources are made available too easily. If, for whatever reason, a project appeals strongly to someone, then that person can easily request permission to start if they achieve a low cost estimate. During the development of the project they can acquire additional resources with the argument that if they don't get them the initial resources will be wasted. This game is sometimes successfully played at government level (for example, Concorde!) and in enterprise.

This dilemma can be solved by always making both calculations (i.e. with and without the costs already incurred) and thoroughly investigating the reason why the first analysis was too optimistic. Financial returns that have been too lightly assessed should clearly be penalized. A researcher who is technically highly qualified but cannot assess is on balance but a mediocre employee.

Apart from possible sanctions, such an investigation serves to check to what extent the new analyses are in fact reliable. If they are not, it might be wiser to cut off the project in order to prevent the creation of white elephants. At the beginning of this chapter it was stated that methods for financial return analysis are merely assessments, despite the apparent exactness of the calculations. This fact should always be kept in mind, together with the numerous opportunities for manipulation which result from the uncertainty of the figures. Anyone who has to assess a financial return analysis should therefore pay as much attention to the underlying assumptions as to the final figure.

Moreover, in order to foster consistency in those assumptions it is advisable to have one person in the enterprise methodically following the realization of the financial return analysis. They can also provide support and guidance for those who have to analyse the financial return so that this analysis takes as short a time as possible.

Although the entries for the financial return form have to be completed by various departments it is highly advisable to have it done by a team. Through their combined effort each department gains a clearer insight into the opinions about the project prevailing in other departments and views can be exchanged.

On page 3 it was pointed out how valuable methods for investment selection are in analysing the consequences of project changes and both pleasant and unpleasant surprises can result. When, in analysing the financial return of an investment project, more than one alternative is calculated, it is called a sensitivity analysis. A sensitivity analysis can be most useful. One may go one step further and use stochastic variables in an analysis of the financial return, in which, apart from an estimate of gross sales, an indication is given of the reliability of the estimate. With the aid of this reliability analysis the reliability of, for example, the given net present value can be calculated. Such techniques appear in most text-books,[9] but this author has never come across them in practice.

At the end of this section the point is made that the discussion, method and examples in this chapter are all related to the financial return before financing. This means that the financial appeal of the project itself is analysed. The project can be made more appealing through good financing and consequently the financial return on the money invested by the shareholders can be assessed. This is called financial return after financing (see Annexe 5). In case proceeds from royalties are received, for example, when an enterprise establishes a subsidiary that has to pay for the parental know-how, then an integral cost-benefit analysis can be made, taking these proceeds (possibly after allowing for taxes) into consideration. In order to get an idea of whether the project itself is sound, however, financial return before financing is the only correct criterion.

The method

The method has been summarized below in a way that can be comprehended by readers who have omitted the previous theory. The method will be dealt with step by step with reference to the form for financial return analysis (Table 2.6).

Step 1

(a) Assess the research costs for each year. In case the research costs are not converted into assets (applicable to by far the majority of projects) enter the costs on line b. If the research costs are in fact converted into assets, they will have to be entered on line k.
(b) Assess the likelihood of success for each year that the project is in research. Write these figures (as figures between zero and one) on lines c or m respectively.
(c) Assess the fictional research costs for each year from lines b_1 and n.

Remark 1

It might be that research costs will have to be entered both under b and k, but generally this is not the case.

Remark 2

When subsequent research costs are intended for maintenance or improvement they can be entered directly on line b_1. This is the case when the project is running and also, for example, when additional research is being carried out during production.

Step 2

(a) Assess the investment in fixed assets and put it on line o. Possible expansion investment in later years should also be entered.
(b) Assess the annual gross sales (line a) and operational costs (line b_2). Take into account possible amounts for prolonged supporting research and expansion of gross

Table 2.6 Form for financial return analysis

Quantity	Code	Year									
		1	2	3	4	5	6	7	8	9	10
Gross sales	a										
Research costs	b										
Likelihood of success	c										
Fictional research costs	$b_1 = b/c$										
Operational costs	b_2										
Depreciation	$d = 0.2\,(n+o)$										
Income before tax	$e = a - b_1 - b_2 - d$										
Tax	$f = 0.5e$										
ROI-income	$g = e - f$										
Cash flow	$h = g + d$										
Research investment	k										
Likelihood of success	m										
Fictional research investment	$n = k/m$										

Investment fixed assets	o
Expansion working capital	p
Investments	$q = n+o+p$
Cash-flow - investments	$s = h-q$
Same, accumulated	$S = \Sigma s$
Discounting factor	$t = (1+r)^i$
Discounted cash flow (DCF)	$u = s/t$
Net present value	$U = \Sigma u$
Accumulated investments	$Q = \Sigma q$
Accumulated depreciations	$D = \Sigma d$
Invested capital	$v = Q-D$
Return on investment	$w = g/v$

r = discount rate
i = year number

Note: Capital symbols express accumulated values. Negative numbers are in parentheses. Corporation tax is assumed to be 50%.

sales through expansion investments in later years. Licence proceeds or other extra income should be entered on *a* as well. Broadly speaking, the figures in line *a* can be said to represent the marketing department's expectations of the project, whereas line b_2 indicates the expectations of the production. Selling costs should be included under b_2, or subtracted from gross sales *a*.

(c) Now assess the amounts required as working capital and also expansion of the working capital. The latter is entered on line *p*.

Step 3

(a) Calculate line *q*.
(b) Calculate line *d* as a percentage of $(n + o)$; there is no depreciation on expansions of working capital. Depreciate these amounts in five years unless laid down otherwise. The amounts under *d* are the sum of the amounts of 20 per cent of the amounts $(n + o)$. Thus, for example: *d* (in year 5) = 20 per cent of $(n + o)$ (of year 4) + 20 per cent of $(n + o)$ (year 3) + 20 per cent of $(n + o)$ (year 2), etc. This is a business economic depreciation that may deviate from the fiscal depreciation according to enterprise practice.
(c) Calculate line *e* up to and including *h*.
(d) Calculate line *s*.
(e) Calculate line *S*, the accumulated (non-discounted) cash flows.
(f) Calculate the non-discounted pay-back period as the moment at which *S* becomes positive

Step 4

(a) Choose a discount rate *r* (e.g. 15 per cent) and copy the discount factor *t* from Table 2.7.
(b) Calculate the discounted cash flows (line *u*).
(c) Calculate the accumulated discounted cash flow *U*, or the net present value.
(d) Calculate, if required, the discounted pay-back period as the moment at which *U* becomes positive.

Table 2.7 Discounting factors – $t = (1 + r)^i$

r %	Year (i) 1 $(1+r)$	2 $(1+r)^2$	3 $(1+r)^3$	4 $(1+r)^4$	5 $(1+r)^5$	6 $(1+r)^6$	7 $(1+r)^7$	8 $(1+r)^8$	9 $(1+r)^9$	10 $(1+r)^{10}$
1	1.01	1.02	1.03	1.04	1.05	1.06	1.07	1.08	1.09	1.10
2	1.02	1.04	1.06	1.08	1.10	1.13	1.15	1.17	1.20	1.22
3	1.03	1.06	1.09	1.13	1.16	1.19	1.23	1.27	1.30	1.34
4	1·04	1.08	1.12	1.17	1.22	1.27	1.32	1.37	1.42	1.48
5	1.05	1.10	1.16	1.22	1.28	1.34	1.41	1.48	1.55	1.63
6	1.06	1.12	1.19	1.26	1.34	1.42	1.50	1.59	1.69	1.79
7	1.07	1.14	1.23	1.31	1.40	1.50	1.61	1.72	1.84	1.97
8	1.08	1.16	1.26	1.36	1.47	1.59	1.71	1.85	2.00	2.16
9	1.09	1.19	1.30	1.41	1.54	1.68	1.83	1.99	2.17	2.37
10	1.10	1.21	1.33	1.46	1.61	1.77	1.95	2.14	2.36	2.59
11	1.11	1.23	1.37	1.52	1.69	1.87	2.08	2.30	2.56	2.84
12	1.12	1.25	1.40	1.57	1.76	1.97	2.21	2.48	2.77	3.11
13	1.13	1.28	1.44	1.63	1.84	2.08	2.35	2.66	3.00	3.39
14	1.14	1.30	1.48	1.69	1.93	2.19	2.50	2.85	3.25	3.71
15	1.15	1.32	1.52	1.75	2.01	2.31	2.66	3.06	3.52	4.05
16	1.16	1.35	1.56	1.81	2.10	2.44	2.83	3.28	3.80	4.41
17	1.17	1.37	1.60	1.87	2.19	2.57	3.00	3.51	4.11	4.81
18	1.18	1.39	1.64	1.94	2.29	2.70	3.19	3.76	4.44	5.23
19	1.19	1.42	1.69	2.01	2.39	2.84	3.38	4.02	4.79	5.69
20	1.20	1.44	1.73	2.07	2.49	2.99	3.58	4.30	5.16	6.19
21	1.21	1.46	1.77	2.14	2.59	3.14	3.80	4.59	5.56	6.73
22	1.22	1.49	1.82	2.22	2.70	3.30	4.02	4.91	5.99	7.30
23	1.23	1.51	1.86	2.29	2.82	3.46	4.26	5.24	6.44	7.93
24	1.24	1.54	1.91	2.36	2.93	3.64	4.51	5.59	6.93	8.59
25	1.25	1.56	1.95	2.44	3.05	3.81	4.77	5.96	7,45	9.31
26	1.26	1.59	2.00	2.52	3.18	4.00	5.04	6.35	8.00	10.09
27	1.27	1.61	2.05	2.60	3.30	4.20	5.33	6.77	8.59	10.92
28	1.28	1.64	2.10	2.68	3.44	4.40	5.63	7.21	9.22	11.81
29	1.29	1.66	2.15	2.77	3.57	4.61	5.94	7.67	9.89	12.76
30	1.30	1.69	2.20	2.86	3.71	4.83	6.27	8.16	10.60	13.79

Step 5

(a) If the net present value is higher than zero, repeat step 4 with a higher discount rate.

(b) Continue to repeat Step 4 until the discount rate has been found at which the net present value is zero. This is the required internal rate of return.

(c) If required the NPV and/or DPBP can be plotted against the discount rate in order to ascertain the exact IRR by interpolation.

Step 6

In some instances it may be desirable to establish the return on investment (ROI). This is the (yearly changing) ratio between the ROI-income (line g) and the invested capital. This invested capital is equal to the accumulated investment (Q) minus depreciations. Proceed as follows:

(a) Calculate the accumulated investment Q.
(b) Calculate the accumulated depreciation D.
(c) Calculate the invested capital (line v).
(d) Calculate the ROI (line w).

The ROI has not been dealt with in this chapter because it is a means to the post-evaluation of the financial working of the enterprise. As a financial return method it is of less importance because the ROI percentages differ from year to year. Nevertheless, step 6 has been included for the sake of completeness.

Example

We shall now work out an example and, in doing this, follow the 'steps' of the previous section. Use round figures; round 0.5 off upwards; put negative figures between brackets. All data, including expenses, should be presented in positive figures (see Table 2.8).

Step 1

(a) Estimate the research costs for year 1 at \$50 and for year 2 at \$100 (line b). Assume that a figure of \$400 is spent on development work in year 2 and that this amount is converted into an asset (enter on line k).
(b) Estimate this as 0.4 for the first \$50; 0.6 for \$100 and 0.8 for \$400.
(c) Calculate b_1 and n.

Step 2

(a) Assume the investment in fixed assets for year 1 to be \$400, for year 2 \$600.

(b) Suppose the gross sales in year 3 equal $2,000 and assume a yearly increase in this amount of 15 per cent (line *a*). Estimate the costs in year 3 at $1,500 and assume a yearly increase of 10 per cent (line b_2).

(c) Estimate the required working capital at 30 per cent of the gross sales. This yields a figure of $600 in year 3 (line *p*) and after that a constant 30 per cent of the expansion in gross sales.

Step 3

a and *b*: no problems. Depreciate in five years according to the instruction.
c, d and *e* no details; *f*: *S* becomes positive in year 7, to be exact after six years and eight months. This is the non-discounted pay-back period. Sometimes the start of the operations is decisive in calculating the pay-back period. In the example this moment is at the beginning of year 3, rendering the pay-back period, according to this definition, equal to four years and eight months.

Step 4

First, choose a discount rate of 15 per cent. This yields an NPV of $206 and a discounted pay-back period of nine years and two months.

Step 5

(a) This discount rate is obviously too low. Now choose 20 per cent. This yields an NPV of minus $99 and a DPBP of over ten years.

(b) The internal rate of return has to be in between these two values and can be found graphically by interpolation. This interpolation is shown in Figure 2.2. If a straight line is drawn between $r = 15$ per cent and $r = 20$ per cent, the point of intersection is $r = 18.3$ per cent. However, it is no use calculating the IRR to three decimal places, because figures have been rounded off and, in addition, such an (apparent) exactness serves no purpose. A calculation with $r = 18$ per cent yields an

Table 2.8 Worked example

Quantity	Code	Year 1	2	3	4	5	6	7	8	9	10
Gross sales	a	–	–	2,000	2,300	2,645	3,042	3,498	4,023	4,626	5,320
Research costs	b	50	100								
Likelihood of success	c	0.4	0.6								
Fictional research costs	$b_1 = b/c$	125	167								
Operational costs	b_2	–	–	1,500	1,650	1,815	1,997	2,196	2,416	2,657	2,923
Depreciation	$d = 0.2\ (n+o)$	–	80	300	300	300	300	220	–	–	–
Income before tax	$e = a - b_1 - b_2 - d$	(125)	(247)	200	350	530	745	1,082	1,607	1,969	2,397
Tax	$f = 0.5e$	(63)	(124)	100	175	265	373	541	804	985	1,199
ROI-income	$g = e - f$	(62)	(123)	100	175	265	372	541	803	984	1,198
Cash-flow	$h = g + d$	(62)	(43)	400	475	565	672	761	803	984	1,198
Research investment	k	–	400								
Likelihood of success	m	–	0.8								
Fictional research investment	$n = k/m$	–	500								
Investment fixed assets	o	400	600								
Expansion working capital	p	–	–	600	90	104	119	137	158	181	208
Investments	$q = n + o + p$	400	1,100	600	90	104	119	137	158	181	208

Cash-flow - investments	$s = h - q$	(462)	(1,143)	(200)	385	461	553	624	645	803	990
Same, accumulated	$S = \Sigma s$	(462)	(1,605)	(1,805)	(1,420)	(959)	(408)	216	861	1,664	2,654
Discounting factor	$t = (1+r)^i$	1.15	1.32	1.52	1.75	2.01	2.31	2.66	3.06	3.52	4.05
		1.20	1.44	1.73	2.07	2.49	2.99	3.58	4.30	5.16	6.19
Discounted cash-flow (DCF)	$u = s/t$	(402)	(866)	(132)	2,200	229	239	235	211	228	244
		(385)	(794)	(116)	186	185	185	174	150	156	160
Net present value	$U = \Sigma u$	(402)	(1,268)	(1,400)	(1,180)	(951)	(712)	(477)	(266)	(38)	206
		(385)	(1,179)	(1,295)	(1,109)	(924)	(739)	(565)	(415)	(259)	(99)
Accumulated investments	$Q = \Sigma q$	400	1,500	2,100	2,190	2,294	2,413	2,550	2,708	2,889	3,097
Accumulated depreciations	$D = \Sigma d$	–	80	380	680	980	1,280	1,500	1,500	1,500	1,500
Invested capital	$v = Q - D$	400	1,420	1,720	1,510	1,314	1,133	1,050	1,208	1,389	1,597
ROI	$w = g/v$ (%)	–	–	6	12	20	33	52	66	71	75

r = discount rate
i = year number

Note: Capital symbols identify accumulated values. Negative amounts are in parentheses. It is assumed that the corporation tax rate is 50% i.e. $f = 0.5e$

NPV of $6. This almost equals zero, which leads us to the conclusion that the IRR is equal to 18 per cent.

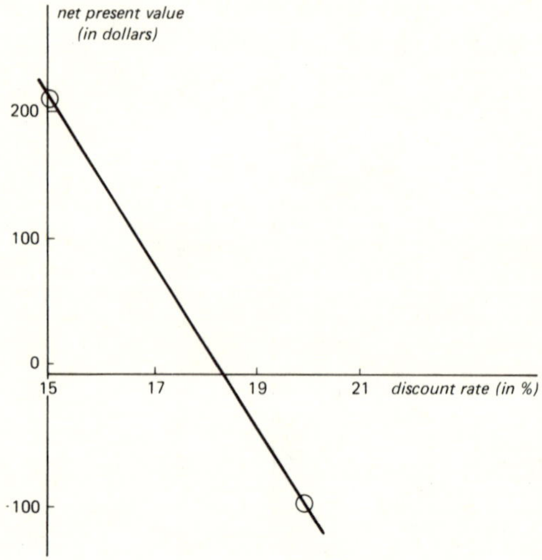

Figure 2.2 Net present value against discount rate of example

Step 6

Finally, for the sake of completeness, the ROI-values have been calculated. As is to be expected, these percentages will rise very high when the project has been depreciated and the profits are only charged with the expansion of the working capital as an investment.

Summary

In order to assess the future financial return of an investment project three methods have been discussed, namely:

pay-back period (with or without discounted cash flows);
net present value;
internal rate of return.

With the help of a standard form these three data can easily be calculated. An example of the use of the form has been given. Special attention has been paid to the input of the research and development costs (R&D) and the input of the development risk. The commercial risk can be assessed through a sensitivity analysis.

Calculating the pay-back period suffices to get a quick, surface impression of the financial appeal. A more profound judgement requires calculation of the net present value, the internal rate of return and preferably an equivalence curve. If there is an option between projects the net present value method should be applied.

3. SYNERGY AND AFFINITY TO STRATEGY

Introduction

The terms synergy and strategy have been amply dealt with in Chapter 1, so the following short definitions will suffice:

> *Synergy is the advantage that emerges from the combination of activities, and affinity to strategy is the extent to which an investment project fits in with the set objectives or parts of them.*

Before we set about developing a method of assessing synergy and affinity to strategy we shall first have to deal with the term 'objectives'. It is a household word in management science and because objectives are different in kind there is often a great deal of misunderstanding.

Objectives

We start our taxonomy by distinguishing general and specific objectives. General objectives determine the company's direction; they are not guidelines for action. Specific objectives do have operational value: they have been derived from general objectives and for the rest depend on internal and external circumstances.

General objectives have two dimensions, namely an income-generating and an income-spending dimension, in other words; striving for a high income versus striving for a good life. In the policy of a major Dutch building company these objectives have been formulated thus: 'Our activities are being carried out in order to continually ensure: (i) a source of income for our personnel and shareholders; (ii) opportunities for the personal development of our employees' talents.'

This conflict between the two major objectives creates a continual problem of choice in all levels of the company and could equally be the actions of individuals, families, enterprises and countries, since all these groups have the same problem of choice, and vacillate between the two general objectives.

For a company the two general objectives can be described as follows:

(i) striving for income-generating continuity; this can be achieved by capital growth and continuity of capital;
(ii) striving for a good social working climate, development opportunities for employees, good working conditions, workers' participation, etc.

When the financial results of the company are bad, the emphasis will be on the first objective, on penalty of the company's bankruptcy. When results are satisfactory the pressure for better social conditions will increase and the emphasis is shifted to the second general objective. The same applies to individuals or nations. This leads to a development path represented schematically in Figure 3.1.

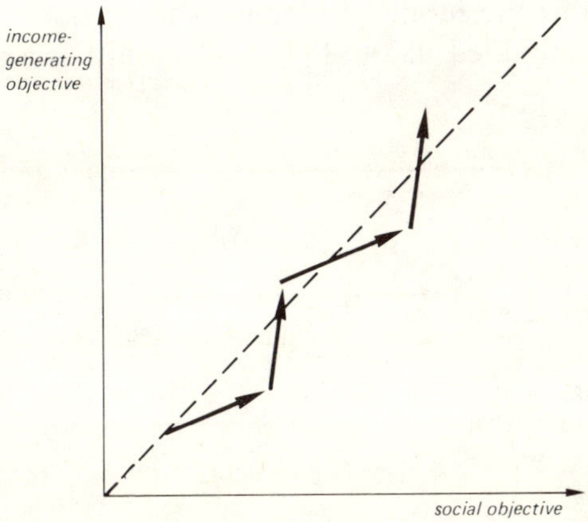

Figure 3.1 Schematic development path of people, companies and nations, with alternating emphasis on the dimensions of the general objectives

Levels of objective

Companies and other organizations attempt to realize their general objectives through certain strategies; such a strategy is thus at the same time the objective of the sub-level. We shall clarify this by means of an example for an individual. Suppose someone requires easy mobility for his particular life style. The means to realize his objective is, in this case, to have a car at his disposal. There are several strategies for getting a car: to buy one (new or second-hand), to borrow, to use a company car, etc. When the strategy to acquire a car has been successful our individual then has as his objective, say, a five-year life-span for the car. The means to this end are maintenance and a garage. From this point on several strategies are possible, i.e. spend a lot of money on a garage and hope there will be few maintenance costs, or take a chance and suffer possible maintenance costs.This example has been represented in the figure below. The general objective (moving about easily) is achieved by choosing a strategy. The strategy chosen in our example is: buying a second-hand car. When the car has been bought it leads to a specific objective: its life-span should be five years. In order to realize this objective there is another choice between various strategies; in this example the choice was renting a garage.

Where does the money for the car and garage come from? This is not included in the figure because it is a sub-strategy

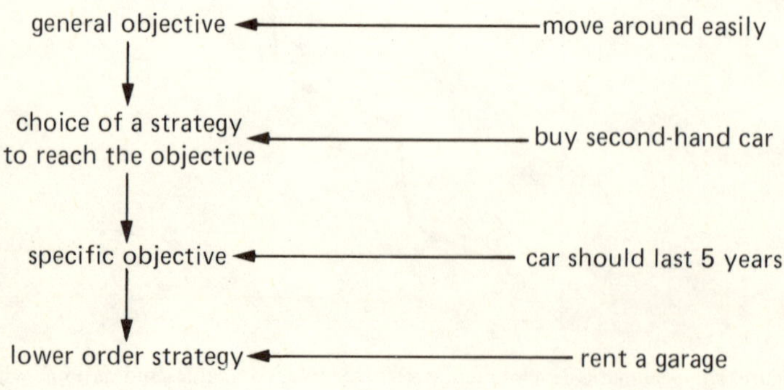

Figure 3.2 The hierarchy of objectives and their relationship with strategies

to the general income-generating strategy. The person in question can aim to earn a certain amount of money per year, and consequently choose a strategy to achieve his objective. In this way a similar hierarchy can be set up for both the income-generating objective and the income-spending objective.

Corporate objectives

A company also achieves its general objectives through strategies which in turn lead to specific objectives. The general income-generating objective consists of three types of specific objectives, namely:

corporate objectives;
objectives of product/market combinations (PMCs) or business units;
objectives of functional departments (FD objectives).

The corporate objectives represent the objectives of the company in its totality with regard to the desired mix of activities. An example of a corporate objective might be the desired geographical spread of the business. A Dutch entrepreneur once explained that he wished to realize one-third of his gross sales in the Netherlands, one-third in the rest of Europe and one-third in the rest of the world, of which latter part the main bulk should be in the United States. This kind of geographical objective can also be formulated in terms of invested capital spreading or profit sharing.

Another example of a corporate objective is the limitation of business activities: 'what business are we in?' A chemical plant will seldom produce the entire spectrum of chemicals. Are the business's activities limited to resins, plastics, solvents, inorganic substances? Do they include pharmacy or paints?

Another example is the desired number of 'legs we stand on'. A Swedish entrepreneur once came to the Netherlands in search of attractive licences, with the following philosophy: his company consisted of two divisions both dealing in a combination of pharmaceutical products. The company had its own trade marks and had invested heavily in the market.

The entrepreneur was primarily looking for licences that would constitute a 'third leg to stand on'. In acquiring these licences he was willing to enter into long-term obligations and to invest in depth in market and production. His requirement was that these activities could grow within five years into an undertaking whose gross sales and profits could be compared to each of the existing divisions. He feared the prospect of the giant-and-many-dwarfs type of company. Apart from his search for licences that would fit in with his strategy he was not averse to a few profitable sidelines. But the pay-back period of these had to be very short; he marketed them under the existing trade mark and if something went wrong he could easily drop them.

Other types of corporate objectives are: are we a manufacturing or a trading company, or both? How far should backward integration extend (this means producing one's own raw materials, possibly up to natural resources such as oil, coal, ore, clay, agricultural raw materials) and how far forward integration (distributing and selling one's own products up to the final consumer)? What is the maximum acceptable vulnerability to seasonal or economic cycles?

Thus, corporate objectives reflect the limitations of the business activities, their desired mix and their desired cohesion.

PMC objectives

We define a business unit or product/market combination (PMC) as a group of more or less homogeneous or corresponding business activities that can be regarded as a strategic unit of the enterprise. From a strategic point of view PMCs can be measured in two ways. First, an attempt can be made to establish which product-life cycle phase each PMC is in. Next, the PMC's competitive power can be established, the latter, naturally, in relation to the competitive power of companies operating in the same market segment. When we check both dimensions against each other the familiar strategic grid[10] is formed, in which PMC strategies can be visualized. Neither the grid nor the way in which PMCs are defined will be dealt with in this book.[11] What we are concerned with here is that the objective of a PMC is its competitive power. There is much confusion about this still. Some companies say: the objective of this PMC is to realize x dollars turnover, or y dollars profit contribution, in year z. This is not an objective but a derivative of the objective. Formerly, in the days of long-range planning, such an approach was considered to be an objective. Now that we try to think more strategically the objective of a PMC is its desired long-term competitive power. This can be expressed in two ways:

> in terms of market shares. The objective of PMC *X* is, say, a share of 20 per cent; the objective of *Y*, 40 per cent;
>
> in terms of ranking. With PMC *X* we want to be the best on the U.K. market and in Germany we do not want more than three other companies to be better than we are; with *Y* we want to be number two in all markets.

For some PMCs the strategy will be: expansion of the market share (or to be higher up the league table). The aim of other PMCs may be to maintain the market share or even to accept a decrease. In addition to these three there are three other PMC strategies (there are six in all), which have been described elsewhere.[12] Once a certain strategy has been decided upon the future gross sales can be assessed, allowing for the expected market development.

In combination with an estimate of the sales/price and cost analysis a profit prognosis can be drawn up. If this profit prognosis is not acceptable another strategy has to be opted for and another profit prognosis has to be drawn up. Thus, a PMC strategy is established by trial and error. This definition is equally applicable in small companies. The objective of a retailer may be a certain net income and from that objective the retailer assesses his requisite turnover. Yet, he too is trying to conquer or defend a market share, even if it is at a local level. The term 'market' should be defined on a local scale in such cases; another district for the shopkeeper is equivalent to another country for the multinational. The only exceptions to this rule that the objective of a PMC is the the desired competitive power are public utilities (gas, water, electricity) and non-competitive markets (agriculture and horticulture). The objective here is the same as that of any government service industry monopoly: for a clarification of this subject the reader is referred to p. 59 in this book.

Functional department objectives

Finally, we come to the policy of the functional departments (FD, sometimes also called company sectors). By this term we mean the sales organization, production, buying department, research, social policy, management policy, etc., in short the functions that allow business activities to be performed. For the larger part these departments have a service function towards the PMC objectives and their objectives are derivatives from the PMC's objectives. But an FD objective is more than the sum of the relevant parts of the PMC objectives. A sales organization in a given country will have its own objectives, for example, with regard to the minimal gross sales in that country that are required to form the basis of an effective sales organization. If the PMC's combined sales effort in that country is too low the FD sales will force the PMC to become more active. In addition, research projects will be carried out that do not issue from the PMC objectives or corporate objectives, i.e. activities aimed at enhancing its own efficient operation.[13]

Strategic planning

In Figure 3.3 the coherence between the various objectives has been visualized. Each organization's first objectives are general objectives, including a weighing of the income-generating objectives against the income-spending or social objectives. This often results in a broad statement that can be used for any other organization with very few adjustments.

The issues will be clarified by the specific objectives, which can be divided into three types. This triangle of specific objectives depends both on the income-generating objectives and the social objectives. The relationship with the social objectives is strongest in the social policy FD. In practice, the objectives in Figure 3.3 can be conflicting. There will always be a conflict between the income-generating objectives (making money) and the social objectives (the good life). In

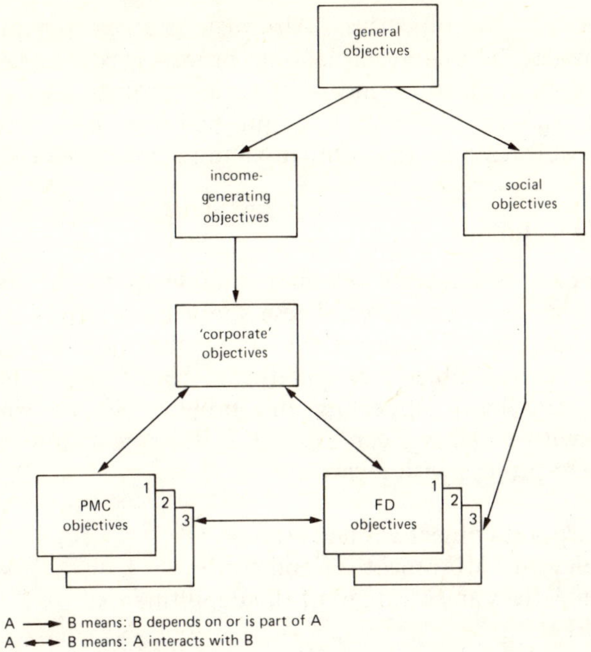

N.B. FD objective 3 stands for the objectives of the functional department for social policy

Figure 3.3 Taxonomy of objectives

addition, there are conflicts within the triangle of specific objectives. If a given PMC wants to expand its market share in France, whereas the corporate objective is to enlarge the percentage of invested capital in the United States, there is obviously a conflict. In this way conflicts with the FDs may also occur, for example, with the financing function (healthy financial ratios for the future, as against 'we need money now'). The various FDs within the enterprise responsible for formulating and realizing the various objectives (this responsibility may rest with departments, sub-organizations, committees, managers, in a variety of forms which will not be dealt with in this book) will have to bring the objectives in line, otherwise the organization cannot be properly run. A synthesis will be achieved by the use of strategic planning methods.[14] Strategic planning is the means by which the organization formulates its objectives, and its most important strategies – the combined activities that should lead to a realization of the objectives. Although strategic planning is considered to be mainly a planning process it is in fact much more a communication and information process. One could say that strategic planning is the internal negotiating process over the objectives of the company and its component parts.

A profile technique

The process of strategic planning thus leads to the formulation of specific objectives. These specific objectives are the check points for investment decisions: the more an investment meets the objectives and the more affinity it has to strategy, the more appealing the project. So we want a method with which we can assess the strategic affinity of an investment project with regard to:

- the corporate objectives and strategy;
- the relevant PMC objectives and strategy;
- the objectives and strategy of the departments:
  - marketing;
  - production;
  - purchasing;
  - R&D;
  - finance;
  - personnel;
  - management development.

Moreover, we want to assess the synergy of the project with the seven departments concerned. In contrast to the financial return analysis, expressing synergy and affinity to strategy in figures has little operational value. This obscures the second investment criterion, because, for example, one project can score high in production and low in personnel. whereas another can be just the reverse. Both instances would give the same (average) figure, which would suggest that both projects are equally appealing, whereas totally different activities are in fact at stake.

We have therefore chosen a profile technique in which a keyword represents the affinity to strategy and synergy of each of the nine aspects mentioned above. The affinities to strategy and synergy are entered in the profile by means of an *X* and an *O* respectively (see Table 3.1).

How should such a profile be read? Table 3.1 summarizes a project that is very desirable from a PMC point of view. The synergy with marketing is good, which means that the project can easily be included in the present marketing activities. It is, however, no great challenge to the marketing organization, which apparently wants to develop in another direction than the one needed for this project. So, affinity to marketing strategy scores low, though not negatively. If it did it would mean that the project would jeopardize the desired development of the marketing organization.

Table 3.1 Example of a strategy/synergy profile

	Negative	None	Weak	Moderate	Strong
Corporate		O		X	
PMC					X
Marketing			X	O	
Production				OX	
Purchasing				OX	
R&D		O			X
Finance				OX	
Personnel			O		X
Management				OX	

X = affinity to strategy
O = synergy
OX = coincidence of *X* and *O*

For the R&D department the project opens up new possibilities in a most desirable direction, and for the personnel department it offers new opportunities as well. For the other sectors, it provides a good fit, but offers little challenge. Assessing the profile points is carried out by means of gradation and keywords. There are four gradations (none, weak, moderate and strong), with the possibilty of signalizing a negative synergy or affinity to strategy. The latter is the case when realizing the project means an adverse effect on the chosen strategy instead of a reinforcing effect and/or the synergy within the functional sector is decreasing instead of increasing. This may be the case when the new project actually forces the sector to choose a new organization structure, which is less opportune for that sector in itself. When the project goes through the disadvantages for this sector are obviously considered not to outweigh the advantages for the other sectors of the PMC and corporate policy.

Assessing the corporate or PMC synergy is related to the mutual coherence at corporate and PMC level. For both levels this synergy is to a greater extent included in the synergy with the functional aspects. For consolidation of mutual coherence is mostly related to better collective activities of the sales, production, purchasing and other departments. However, a few questions remain to be answered at corporate level: for instance, the possibility of captive use (see p. 56 for an explanation), a better utilization of holding companies or subsidiary companies abroad, and maybe others. These aspects belong for the most part to synergy, cannot be included in the functional aspects, and therefore justify a corporate-synergy-entry in the profile. Since the PMC synergy appears to be realized within the functional departments we have not included a PMC synergy entry.

Preparing the profile

Each entry in the profile is found from the answer to a number of questions. Since there are nine strategic items and eight synergistic objectives, there are seventeen questionnaires. The questions in these questionnaires are a direct translation from the specific objectives. This conversion is crucial for the second investment criterion: objectives are check points for investment decisions and are translated into strategy/synergy questions, the answers to which can be visualized in a profile. Examples of these questionnaires have been included at the end of this chapter. The answers to the questions will have to be given in the keywords, negative, none, weak, moderate, strong, in the same way as in the profile itself. The strategy or synergy point on the profile is the weighted average of the answers to the questions corresponding to that point.

An example: Suppose we are assessing the synergy with production with the help of five questions. A group has given answers to each of the five questions (see Table 3.2). Subsequently, suppose that the group consider questions *b* and *c* to be of greater importance than the other questions. This is indicated by allotting 'weights' – 100 points spread over the questions – giving an indication of the importance of the question. In the example *b* and *c* get 30 points, *a* and *e*, and *d* 20 points. Together this totals 100. The sum of the weights should always be 100, otherwise the final calculation does not tally. For the sake of the 'score' the keywords are translated into figures. 'Negative' gets 10 points, 'none' 20 points, etc. Multiplication of weights and scores gives the weighted scores:

$$\text{weighted score} = \frac{\text{weight} \times \text{score}}{100}$$

Summation of the weighted scores gives a number (39 in the example) that is to be translated into the nearest keyword ('moderate' in the example, since 39 is nearest to 40). The profile point for 'synergy with production' will thus be 'moderate'.

Table 3.2 The establishment of a profile point: synergy with production

Question	Negative (10)	None (20)	Weak (30)	Moderate (40)	Strong (50)	Weight	Score	Weighted
a		•				10	20	2
b			•			30	30	9
c					•	30	50	15
d					•	20	50	10
e			•			10	30	3
						–		–
Total						100		39

The questions that have been formulated as an example on the following pages obviously differ from organization to organization. They require lengthy discussion before they can be formulated as they represent the organization's specific objectives. An organization should at one time, however, choose a final set of questions. In order to compare how the projects differ between themselves the questions must not be altered afterwards.

The weights for each question must also be established because for every project the same weights should be used for comparison's sake. Both weights and questions emerge from strategic policy, since in that policy the relative importance of the various aspects should be established. Users of the method are advised not to be afraid of giving relatively large weights, e.g. 50 or 60, to one question. Failure to do this tends to result in 'moderate' answers for all projects. The profile technique is devised to contrast the projects and the failure to give relatively large weights to one question makes it a blunt instrument.

Filling in the questionnaires

For the strategic/synergistic analysis it is essential to have the questionnaires filled in by a multi-functional group of people. This can be realized as follows: from each sector two people are invited to co-operate in the analysis, one of them closely connected to the development of the project and the other senior in the sector but somewhat more remote from the development. Those sectors not so closely involved in the project should send one person only. They should be adequately informed beforehand of both the objective and the relevant aspects of the project.

After this introduction and discussion each of the participants fills in the first questionnaire. Next, all the answers are read aloud and grouped together on a flip-chart. When the answers are quite similar, the average answer of the participants to each question can be ascertained, and hence the profile point calculated. When one or two answers are widely divergent, further discussion is required.

It will appear that these discussions are at least as important as the end profile itself. The strategic/synergistic analysis is a powerful agent of communication since discussions are being provoked which result in various points of view being clarified and a consensus being reached.

After the discussions and the agreed consensus the next questionnaire is filled in until the profile is completed. Experience has taught that this takes from half to one day per project. The result of this way of working is a careful balancing of each other's points of view, giving a motivated profile, thus simplifying the high-level decision-making.

Explanatory notes to the questionnaires

The questions in the questionnaires included in this chapter are all related to a product. Where necessary this should be changed into a process (e.g. production process) or technique. The questionnaire remains the same in the case of a social technique such as function classification or quality circles. The questionnaires need adjustment when used by a non-profit-making organization. Also, non-profit-making organizations have the triangle of specific objectives, but may have less or different functional departments.

The first questionnaire refers to corporate strategy. The corporate strategy is a derivative of the corporate objectives and aims at creating a well-balanced and sound PMC mix for the future. The first two questions on diversification and internationalization reflect this. The third question is aimed at appreciating new activities, closely connected to the products from the so-called 'strategic range'. This question results from the company's objective to strengthen these PMCs in particular in a qualitative and quantitative way. The fourth question deals with joint ventures. In this question joint ventures are considered to go beyond the narrow PMC interest. If this is the case it is of strategic importance on the corporate level. The next two questions are self-evident. It should be emphasized that the inclusion of a question does not necessarily mean that this question is considered to be of importance for the company. When there is no need for diversification at corporate level the first question's weight will be low, whereas the weight of the third question will be very high. On the other hand, when the company opts for a strategy that gives preference to diversification projects and only in the second instance considers strengthening the current strong products, this will be reflected by a high weight for the first question and a relatively low weight for the third question. Hence, it is the weights that reflect the corporate strategy the company has chosen.

The second form gives the two questions mentioned before about synergy at a corporate level. The first question refers to a possible increase in 'captive use', the use of raw materials or end-products, manufactured by the company itself. The second question deals with the utilization of holding companies or subsidiaries, as in the case of multinationals. If no such organizations form part of the company this question can be left out, or given a zero weight, which is the same thing.

The third form is a questionnaire for the PMC strategy. The appeal of the product is now being considered from the point of view of the person responsible for the PMC's profit. These questions are twofold. First, the question is asked as to whether the product will fit in with the chosen PMC strategy. Second, the advantages and potential advantages that have not yet been taken into account in the financial return analysis are explored.

Next, the project is considered from the point of view of the functional managers. They judge the project according to the responsibility they have for a smooth-running operation. They ask themselves this question: from the corporate's and PMC's point of view the project is appealing, but what good will it do for my department?

The questionnaire 'strategy marketing' is derived from a company, distinguishing two market-types: home markets and export markets. The home markets have their own marketing organization and their own labels, export markets do not always have their own label and agents are used. This leads to four objectives:

expansion of the number of export markets;
strengthening of position in export markets;
conversion of export markets into home markets;
strengthening of position in home markets.

The first and third questions are strategic ones; they have therefore been included in the strategy marketing questionnaire. The two other questions have been included in the third question of the synergy marketing questionnaire.

Other questions in the synergy marketing questionnaire refer to the extent to which the product can be utilized to strengthen the marketing department in the desired direction and the desired developments concerning its quality image and to the question whether the product brings about a market differentiation, leading to a more susceptible market for the company's approach.

The questions in the synergy marketing questionnaire require little explanation, except that the penultimate question can also produce a negative answer. A positive answer to this question means a strengthening of the market position because a package of products can be offered. An example of a negative effect was the selling by greengrocers of meat delicacies, leading as it did to a strong reaction from butchers, who started to sell coffee (the so-called 'butchers' coffee' effect). So the meat delicacies did strengthen the greengrocer's package, but exercised a negative effect on the sales of another product. Had this effect been anticipated, the fourth question in the synergy marketing questionnaire should have been answered in the negative.

The questionnaires for production and purchasing require little explanation. The strategy questions deal with possible improvements or strengthening of the organization arising from the new product. The synergy questions refer to the extent to which the product fits in with the existing organization and its contribution towards lower cost prices, other than those included in the financial return analysis. If a new product leads to a decrease in overhead expenses of the existing production facilities this will have been included in the financial return analysis. Should such an advantage be too speculative to be expressed in firm figures the effect should be included in the synergy questionnaires.

The first R&D strategy question deals with the extent to which the product will contribute towards an increase in the specific know-how of a kind desired by the company. The R&D manager needs to know whether the know-how to be developed, apart from possible PMC profits, could be part of the company's future required know-how position. Another strategic question is: can the know-how be patented? This should almost always be striven for. The strategic question of a possible joint venture concerning know-how has not been included in the R&D strategic questionnaire because it has already been included in the corporate questionnaire. The third question in the R&D synergy questionnaire deals with the effect on the people employed and the means by which they will have to be recruited for the project and the impetus of the project itself on the employees' motivation. Sometimes the project requires specialists who have little affinity with the other employees and so there is little spin-off effect. In other cases this may be quite the reverse, leading to the realization, through hindsight, that this has been an important side-effect of the product, apart from the benefit derived from the extra facilities for the product or the product itself.

In the finance questionnaires it is definitely not the financial return that is at stake. The synergy finance questionnaire deals with the extent to which the project can be financed from the means available at a relatively low risk. If there is money available for the project, only a relatively moderate part of the available budget is required and the financial risks are acceptable, the financial synergy score will be high. The strategy finance questions refer to the extent to which the project contributes towards acquiring new financial know-how or access towards new financial sources and also the extent to which the project contributes towards realization of financial objectives such as ROI, ratio equity/borrowed capital, growth of equity capital, interest coverage, etc. If necessary these objectives can be formulated in separate questions.

The questionnaires on personnel and management require no further explanation.

Utilization by non-profit-making organizations, small enterprises and banks

At this point we want to emphasize that the questionnaires are only examples. The functional departments used in the example will not be the same for each and every company or organization; a trading company may not have a production department but it will have departments for transshipment or storage, for example.

So, for each organization the decision will have to be made on:

> which questionnaires will have to be drawn up;
> what questions will have to be included in each questionnaire.

In doing this, possible misunderstandings should be avoided, amongst other things by always formulating positive questions. In non-profit-making organizations, it is true, there are no product/market combinations; however, various types of service (or production) to various customers can be distinguished. So, activity areas can be distinguished, being the equivalent of the company's PMCs. The objectives of these activity areas cannot be expressed in terms of market share or ranking; for example, many government activities are monopolies. In such instances the objectives can be expressed in absolute or relative terms, just as companies do, absolute in the sense of, for instance: 'Our costs are never to exceed two-thirds of inflation', or: 'We will keep our employment at the present level'. In a relative sense the PMC objective may be formulated as: 'Our municipal cleansing department should rank among the cheapest ten such departments', or: 'Our telephone charges should be among the lowest three such services in Europe'. Both examples provide a clear equivalent of competitive power.

To summarize: within a non-profit-making organization there are no PMCs, only activity areas. This requires different definitions of PMC objectives and corporate objectives. The number and characteristics of the functional departments require adjustment, just as the relevant questions do. With these adjustments the method can be used for non-profit-making organizations.

Small enterprises or organizations will probably find the thought behind the method appealing, but the profile method-with-questionnaires too complicated or too much like red tape. Although the latter is not inherent in the method, but in the way it is used, the shortened procedure may be advisable in such cases. To this end, three options are open (compare the shortened version of the first section of Chapter 5):

- Omit the questionnaires. Ask directly: how does this project fit in with the marketing strategy? and enter the result directly as a profile point on the profile.
- Omit a number of profile points. Maybe the corporate points are not appealing or the social and management questions are less applicable. Omitting these points results in a concise profile.
- Omit the distinction between synergy and affinity to strategy. Some think this distinction very abstract; they prefer the direct question: 'How does the R&D department look at the project?'

Although it is obvious that the latter omission especially renders the instrument rather blunt, it is better to start with a blunt instrument than with none at all, allowing for some refinements at a later date, when more experience has been gathered.

Finally, a few words about the use by banks or others who have to judge the appeal of an investment project, for example subsidizers, investment companies, etc. From research at the Graduate Business School it appeared that those external financiers are especially concerned with the expected financial return and the question of whether the management can handle it (thus, the management synergy profile point). The question of whether the management, based on previous experience, is trustworthy, predominates. Banks, for that matter, will often require a security for their loan, in the sense that, for example, fixed assets will be pledged as a security. Banks tend not to explore the other considerations covered here because they think they are not able to judge them. We consider this a rather strange way of looking at things. If banks were prepared to consider their loans more methodically their risks would be limited. That is why we consider that banks had better ask the borrower for a strategy/synergy profile apart from the financial return analysis. Pricking the bubble of would-be arguments about this profile resembles the way it is done in the financial return analysis.

Summary

The strategic/synergistic investment criterion assesses the extent to which an investment project fits in with the company's strategy and the existing capabilities of the functional sectors. Both estimates can be depicted in a profile by means of keywords. Synergy with existing sectors provides seven points, since we have distinguished seven sectors; in addition to that there is a corporate synergy point. The affinity to strategy is also stated for the seven sectors; apart from that estimates are given for the affinity to the corporate and PMC strategies. Each estimate of these seventeen points (eight synergy and nine strategy) is derived from questionnaires; the weighted answer to the questions corresponds to the profile point. It is essential that the questionnaires are completed by a multi-functional team of experts acting as a group. The mutual exchange of views and the resulting consensus about the investment project is as important an objective of the strategy/synergy analysis as the resulting profile itself. The use of the method by small enterprises, banks and non-profit-making organizations has been dealt with, in the course of which an indication has been given of a shortened procedure, if required.

Questionnaire 1

Profile point: Strategy with: Corporate								
Questions	Negative (10)	None (20)	Weak (30)	Moderate (40)	Strong (50)	Weight	Score	Weighted score
Will the project lead to a new PMC fitting into the desired PMC mix?								
Will the project aid in reaching the desired geographical mix of activities?								
Will the project strengthen a priority PMC?								
Could the project lead to interesting co-operation with other organizations at corporation level?								
Will the project reduce the seasonal or business cycle vulnerability?								
Will the project add to our corporate image?								
Sum:						100		
Conclusion: The keyword is:								

Questionnaire 2

Profile point: Synergy with: Corporate								
Questions	Negative (10)	None (20)	Weak (30)	Moderate (40)	Strong (50)	Weight	Score	Weighted score
Can the project utilize products of our company as raw materials or is there captive use for the project? Will the investment lead to a better utilization of our holding organization in other countries?								
Sum:						100		
Conclusion: The keyword is:								

Questionnaire 3

Profile point: Strategy with: PMC								
Questions	Negative (10)	None (20)	Weak (30)	Moderate (40)	Strong (50)	Weight	Score	Weighted score
Will the project contribute to the realization of the desired competitive power? Could the project in principle be used for joint ventures, licence agreements, etc, that have not yet been taken into account in the financial return analysis?								
Sum:						100		
Conclusion: The keyword is:								

Questionnaire 4

Profile point: Strategy with: Marketing								
Questions	Negative (10)	None (20)	Weak (30)	Moderate (40)	Strong (50)	Weight	Score	Weighted score
Will the project stimulate the conversion of the export markets into home markets?								
Can the projects aid in the expansion of the number of export markets?								
Will the project stimulate the planned developments in the marketing department?								
Will the project strengthen the desired developments concerning our quality image?								
Sum:						100		
Conclusion: The keyword is:								

Questionnaire 5

Profile point: Synergy with: Marketing								
Questions	Negative (10)	None (20)	Weak (30)	Moderate (40)	Strong (50)	Weight	Score	Weighted score
Can the project be handled by our present sales and marketing organization? Does the project employ the strengths of our present sales and marketing organization? Does the project provide a long-term basis for our sales and marketing organization or will it strengthen it? Will the project require market investigations that can also be beneficial for other products?								
Sum:	X	X	X	X	X	100	X	
Conclusion: The keyword is:								

Questionnaire 6

Profile point: Strategy with: Production								
Questions	Negative (10)	None (20)	Weak (30)	Moderate (40)	Strong (50)	Weight	Score	Weighted score
Will the project lead to a greater flexibility of our operations? Does the project fit into our requirements for more unique production processes and higher added value? Does the project fit into our requirement for smaller losses in production?								
Sum:						100		
Conclusion: The keyword is:								

Questionnaire 7

Profile point: Synergy with: Production								
Questions	Negative (10)	None (20)	Weak (30)	Moderate (40)	Strong (50)	Weight	Score	Weighted score
Will the project lead to a better utilization of our facilities and/or lower average costs of facilities? Can the project be handled by existing people and facilities? Could the project lead to lower cost prices of other products, other than foreseen in the financial return analysis?								
Sum:						100		
Conclusion: The keyword is:								

Questionnaire 8

Profile point: Strategy with: Purchasing								
Questions	Negative (10)	None (20)	Weak (30)	Moderate (40)	Strong (50)	Weight	Score	Weighted score
Could the project lead to new purchasing know-how or experience that could be beneficial to other products?								
Sum:	X	X	X	X	X	100	X	
Conclusion: The keyword is:								

Questionnaire 9

Profile point: Synergy with: Purchasing								
Questions	Negative (10)	None (20)	Weak (30)	Moderate (40)	Strong (50)	Weight	Score	Weighted score
Could the purchasing be carried out by existing people, facilities and know-how?								
Will the project lead to a better utilization of present people and facilities?								
Will the strong points of the department be utilized?								
Could the project lead to better purchasing conditions for other products, such as quantity discounts?								
Sum:						100		
Conclusion: The keyword is:								

Questionnaire 10

Profile point: Strategy with: R&D								
Questions	Negative (10)	None (20)	Weak (30)	Moderate (40)	Strong (50)	Weight	Score	Weighted score
Will the project lead to unique or specific know-how of a kind desired by our department? Will initiation of the project be difficult, either because of patents or otherwise?								
Sum:						100		
Conclusion: The keyword is:								

Questionnaire 11

Profile point: Synergy with: R&D								
Questions	Negative (10)	None (20)	Weak (30)	Moderate (40)	Strong (50)	Weight	Score	Weighted score
Can the project be developed by existing people and facilities? Will our people and facilities be utilized better? Could the know-how to be developed be beneficial to other projects? Is the know-how to be developed a logical extension of our present capabilities?								
Sum:						100		
Conclusion: The keyword is:								

Questionnaire 12

Profile point: Strategy with: Finance								
Questions	Negative (10)	None (20)	Weak (30)	Moderate (40)	Strong (50)	Weight	Score	Weighted score
Does the product offer opportunities for co-operation with others in financial matters? Does the product contribute significantly to the realization of financial targets?								
Sum:						100		
Conclusion: The keyword is:								

Questionnaire 13

Profile point: Synergy with: Finance				
Questions	Negative (10) None (20) Weak (30) Moderate (40) Strong (50)	Weight	Score	Weighted score
Can the project be financed from available means? Does the project require only a relatively moderate part of the available investment funds? Are the financial risks acceptable? N.B. The answer to this question might come from the sensitivity analysis of the financial return analysis. (Note that the question of financial return itself is not asked in connection with the strategy/synergy profile).				
Sum:	X	100	X	
Conclusion: The keyword is:				

Questionnaire 14

Profile point: Strategy with: Personnel								
Questions	Negative (10)	None (20)	Weak (30)	Moderate (40)	Strong (50)	Weight	Score	Weighted score
Will the project create or ensure jobs? Will the project lead to interesting opportunities for our personnel?								
Sum:						100		
Conclusion: The keyword is:								

Questionnaire 15

Profile point: Synergy with: Personnel								
Questions	Negative (10)	None (20)	Weak (30)	Moderate (40)	Strong (50)	Weight	Score	Weighted score
Can the project be realized with our personnel, i.e. without much extra training?								
Sum:						100		
Conclusion: The keyword is:								

Questionnaire 16

Profile point: Strategy with: Management								
Questions	Negative (10)	None (20)	Weak (30)	Moderate (40)	Strong (50)	Weight	Score	Weighted score
Will the project provide opportunities for improving our management capabilities? (quantitative and/or qualitative) Will the project increase the opportunities for management development? Will the project make our management jobs more attractive to managers?								
Sum:	X	X	X	X	X	100	X	
Conclusion: The keyword is:								

Questionnaire 17

Profile point: Synergy with: Management								
Questions	Negative (10)	None (20)	Weak (30)	Moderate (40)	Strong (50)	Weight	Score	Weighted score
Can the project be realized by presently available managers, i.e. without much extra training?								
Sum:						100		
Conclusion: The keyword is:								

4. SOCIETAL ASPECTS

Introduction

Many enterprises are involved in projects which will have far-reaching societal consequences or in projects which meet with opposition from certain groups. This opposition may be related to environmental, energy or scarcity problems, or to societal issues such as associating with countries which have unacceptable political systems. Although an enterprise cannot always be held responsible for the consequences of a project, it is of the utmost importance to recognize possible societal hurdles at an early stage. If the enterprise has the capacity to do so, the R&D department may develop modifications or alternatives to the project which will meet with less opposition from society. Hence, it is necessary to recognize and minimize societal risk. By societal risk we understand:

- The risk that the project never gets any further than the take-off phase, for reasons other than prices and costs.
- These reasons may be that raw materials, resources, or specific energy supply are scarcer than anticipated; the necessary skilled labour and management are not available; there may be boycotts on selling and purchasing for political reasons, etc.
- The risk of the project having to be thoroughly revised in the growth or consolidation stages of the product-life cycle because environmental or safety standards have been altered or scarcity problems arise.
- The risk of the project reaching the decline phase of the product-life cycle much sooner than anticipated, because brand-new technologies are introduced which have a significantly higher quality-cost ratio; the perception

or consumption pattern of buyers or consumers is changing, or again scarcity, environmental or safety problems.

So the societal interest criterion includes a number of components which have not been taken into account in the financial return analysis or in the synergy and affinity to strategy analysis.

The third investment criterion should answer the question: to what extent does the project link with external social and societal developments and technological progress? Entrepreneurs need to have advance knowledge of these 'hidden threats and opportunities' for two reasons:

- A 'hidden threat' can cause the project suddenly to fail unexpectedly; unexpected opportunities may be overlooked, which result in an unnecessary loss.
- A hidden threat can cause industrial disaster (environment, safety); this lays the moral obligation on each entrepreneur to recognize and avoid these risks as far as possible.

The study of possible societal problems and the optimization of a new technology from a societal point of view is called technology assessment. First we will give a short explanation of this term and then go on to describe a technology assessment method. An evaluation and a summary will conclude this chapter.

What is technology assessment?

Technology assessment is used here to mean a systematic study into the effects on society of the use of a new technology. Its main concern is not so much the primary results, desired and foreseen, as with the (harmful) side-effects, subsequent results, negative reactions and delayed reactions. Since this kind of study is not limited to the technical and economic aspects but also includes ecological, social, psychological, town-planning and, if required, other aspects, it can be said that technology assessment sets itself the ambitious task of investigating the entire problem of the present and future application of a new technology from every possible angle. The term technology should not be interpreted in too narrow a sense. In most languages the use of the term technology is restricted to the scientific study enabling man to turn nature's produce into products to satisfy his needs. The International Society for Technology Assessment defines a technology as 'the practical know-how used in activities that change the natural, social or physical environment of man'. In this sense the know-how of management techniques, the reclaiming of land or the development of a new deodorant are equally included in the definition. The National Academy of Sciences in America puts it like this: 'Technology is a system of interrelated innovations, some technical and some social, comprising some sort of coherent nexus pertaining to systematic manipulation of the environment.'

Ideally, technology assessment should anticipate these consequences and evaluate them with the technology still in progress; hence, it requires a regular look into the future. This is the reason why technology assessment is so close to technology forecasting and those practising both techniques are often one and the same person. Technology assessment has been defined as follows:

Technology assessment is the integral and systematic study into the effects on society of the utilization of a new technology and the pursuit of modifications or alternatives that optimize these effects within the framework of a broad present and future societal interest.[15]

A simple example serves to show the idea of technology assessment. At the turn of the century lead-containing paints were used on a large scale. These paints offered significant advantages as regards coverage and other qualities. It may be assumed that these technical aspects and the economic aspects had been thoroughly considered before the paints were introduced on a large scale.

However, after some time strange paralytic symptoms occurred in people, which could be ascribed, after many tests, to the penetration of the lead into the body, for example, when children put toys with lead paint into their mouths. This discovery led to a very selective use of lead-containing paints. At the present time, however, about

250,000 people in the United States suffer from paralytic symptoms attributed to lead-containing paints. Had a proper technology assessment been made, according to the definition above, this side-effect could have been anticipated and the suffering prevented.

The idea of technology assessment did not receive an equally warm welcome everywhere. In publications we have come across the following expectations:

- First and foremost technology assessment is aimed at investigating the consequences of new technologies from every possible angle. Know-how about the side-effects, otherwise emerging only when the new technology is being applied, would be made available in the development stage.
- On the basis of this broader know-how, a more matter-of-fact discussion between supporters and opponents of the new technology can be expected.
- Through technology assessment the options concerning adjusting and applying new technologies are being uncovered.
- The latter offers the prospect of evaluating alternatives and an early optimization of the technology.

The method

We will now discuss a six-step method for technology assessment.

Step 1

In this first step a number of balances are described for the project. First, a balance is drawn up of all the mass or material components, stating the inflows as well as the outflows of all the goods and materials involved. Mention is made here of such things as cooling water, lubricating oil and packaging material. Since the outflows are listed as well as the inflows, and since the total sums of each of the flows should naturally coincide, the waste flows are also included. The second balance to be drawn up is the energy balance, which should also even out in the end. Which flows of energy (type and quantity) go in and in what form does the energy come out?

In the third balance, the know-how/labour balance, all the various types of know-how and labour needed are summed up, including highly specialized labour, completely unskilled labour, and everything in between, the know-how generated and possibly made available by means of licences, publications, turnover of staff, auxiliary industries, etc. The fourth balance to be drawn up is the financial balance, as has been shown in the financial return analysis.

The fifth and last balance to be drawn up as part of Step 1 is the power or decision-making balance. For each stage of the project one or more public or private licences or permits are necessary. Conversely, the presence of some projects makes other decision-making processes and procedures possible or necessary. It is important to register these processes systematically in order to identify the persons or groups who are involved or dominant in the introduction and use of a technology. Drawing up these five balances may be rather ambitious but it is the only way to find out where the potential dangers or obstacles to the introduction of the new technology lie.

Step 2

Next, the material gathered in Step 1 is centred on tracing the in- and outflows that might either make or receive an impact from society and, consequently, can influence or shape the introduction or growth of the project. Tracing these aspects is done with the help of a check-list for each of the five balances; for the mass or material balance a check-list is given in Table 4.1, for the energy balance in Table 4.2, for the know-how/labour balance in Table 4.3, for the financial balance in Table 4.4 and for the power balance in Table 4.5. A number of aspects that are not specifically covered by any of the balances are traced with the help of Table 4.6.

However, the factors coinciding with the actual introduction of the project are not the only ones that have social consequences; the introduction can also lead to the destruction or replacement of something else, a development

Table 4.1 Mass/material flows

1. List the quantity and composition of all the material inflows and outflows, for:
   - products
   - packaging materials
   - ancillary materials which might be supplied at the same time or at a later date
   - solid waste
   - non-water liquid waste
   - polluted waste water
   - flue gas and burnt gas
   - used cooling water
   - raw materials, ancillary materials and fuels.

2. Do these flows contain components which are:
   - toxic to human beings or the environment?
   - biologically resistant or otherwise non-destructible?
   - detrimental to purification systems?
   - malodorous?
   - irritating to the eyes and/or mucous membranes?
   - inflammable?
   - explosive?
   - carcinogenic
   - costly or scarce?

3. Are there legal restrictions on the use of the materials as components, products or as pertaining to waste disposal (concentration, maximum quantity)?

4. What levies will the project be confronted with? What are the expectations with respect to these levies?

5. How much would a purification system cost? Which purification processes are necessary? Which are suitable? What developments have taken place with respect to the improvement of the purification processes?

6. Do the waste flows contain (scarce) components which can be recycled? Is legislation in existence or anticipated? To what degree will recycling of the product or waste material be possible in the future?

7. Is it anticipated that the waste and by-products released during consumption of the product will have to be taken back from the consumer?

8. Which restrictions and required safety regulations are in existence (and are to be expected) with respect to the transport and storage of the above-mentioned dangerous (toxic, inflammable, explosive, cancer-producing) materials?

9. Is there an unlimited supply of the raw materials and ancillary materials? Is there a chance that these materials will be exclusively reserved for certain purposes, either by the government or by the producer (for example, for private use)?

Table 4.1 Mass/material flows (continued)

Table 4.1 *Continued from page 85*

10. Is there any danger of fire or explosion during the production process? Can substances be released during production which might be dangerous to the workers or other people in the vicinity (for example: intermediate products; substances produced by accidental contact with water vapour, oxygen or carbon dioxide in the air; substances produced by a change in temperature or pressure or by the elimination of a catalyst; or substances produced because materials present in the factory act as catalysts)?

11. How much water is needed and for what purposes? What are the specifications pertaining to the water quality? How is it obtained and how is it discharged? What effect will it have on the ground water level? Is there any danger to the water supply elsewhere? Are there (will there be) any licences necessary or impositions levied? Are any restrictions in existence or expected?

12. How much cooling water has to be discharged? What is its temperature? What are the consequences for the natural environment, for the people who drink this water, for its use as a recreation area?

13. What alternative processes or products are in existence or are feasible requiring less water or milder specifications?

14. Is there another process capable of producing the same product but causing fewer or less serious environmental or raw material problems?

15. Is there another product capable of fulfilling the same functions as the product in question but which can be produced with fewer environmental or raw material problems?

16. What are the advantages in comparison with the alternative products or processes? How can these advantages be utilized in other applications?

Table 4.2 Energy balance

1. Which energy inflows entail a specific form of energy (e.g., various kinds of gas and oil, petroleum, electricity, coal, hot water, hot oil) and for which flows can various types of energy be used?
2. Which primary energy transformations have been planned or are possible (e.g., oil into electricity, coal into hot water, coal into water-gas)?
3. How can energy be saved and how much do the various methods cost? At what energy prices do various ways of saving energy become cost-effective?
4. For every energy outflow, what are the consequences for the natural and social environment? Which consequences can critically influence the development of the technology?
5. Is there another process leading to the same product and using considerably less energy? What considerations led to the selection of this process?
6. Is there another product that can fulfil the same functions as the product in question but requires considerably less energy during its production process?
7. What price changes in each of the primary energy flows have been allowed for?

Table 4.3 Know-how/labour/balance

1. Does the production process involve unpleasant work?
   - physically strenuous
   - high/low temperature
   - high/low humidity
   - dirty
   - dark
   - dusty
   - noisy.
2. Does the production process involve evening shifts, night shifts or weekend shifts?
3. Does the production process involve work with an especially high risk of accidents or illnesses?
4. Is production, maintenance or consumption of the product labour-intensive?
5. Are uncommon or specialized skills needed for production, maintenance, or repairs?
   - product design
   - production sector
   - commercial
   - clerical
   - planning
   - management
   - safety.
6. Which of the above-mentioned skills could also be utilized for other technologies or other versions of the technology in question?

7. What increases in expenses are anticipated with regard to unpleasant, dangerous or specialized labour/know-how?

8. Which alternative processes or products are less dependent on the above-mentioned types of unpleasant, dangerous or specialized labour/know-how?

9. Will use of the new technology significantly alter the international division of labour? Will it cause unemployment in countries with a relatively low standard of living and/or relatively high unemployment?

10. Can the technology be applied to production in developing countries, either for export purposes or for local consumption? In the latter case, are there possibilities for financial or other assistance from developmental aid funds, the World Bank, etc.?

11. Is special know-how needed in the consumption stage? (e.g., programming skills for the use of computers). If so, who will provide this know-how? What will be the social consequences of training (large) groups of experts (e.g., the effect on the demand for preparatory diplomas, the possibility that other diplomas might become obsolete)? Will this expertise be applicable on an international scale?

12. If the new product is not to be used solely by specially trained persons, have the users been sufficiently informed as to the purpose of the product, the consumption process and the waste materials released after consumption? Are written instructions adequate? Are the users aware of the possible dangers from failing to follow the instructions?

13. Can a patent be taken out on the know-how pertaining to the development or the use of the new technology? Can this know-how be sold?

14. Does development of the new technology provide know-how that will alleviate difficulties pertaining to patents in some other field?

Table 4.4 Financial balance

1. Survey all financial inflows and outflows expected over the next ten years and calculate the profit-earning capacity.
2. Are there restrictions, as far as some or all of the funds are concerned, on the choice of financial backers? To what degree can these restrictions influence the introduction of the technology?
3. Is introduction of the technology dependent on subsidies, guarantees or government loans?
4. Which groups will benefit financially from the technology? Which groups can obtain special privileges regarding its use?
5. Will the financiers (whether it is their own investment or on behalf of a second party) demand increased profit rates and other benefits? If so, what and why?
6. Will the loans be able to be supplemented if this proves advisable?
7. What restrictions are there on cash flow to the investors and/or the parties who provide the know-how, and what taxes are charged on this cash flow? Are there restrictions with respect to participation in the share capital of firms which manufacture or sell the product? Can cash flow be transferred abroad?

that can provoke individuals or groups to offer support, issue a protest or claim compensation. Consequently, the question of 'what disappears' is worked out and dealt with in Table 4.7.

It goes without saying that the check-lists given here may be supplemented and improved. It should be noted that some questions do in fact belong to the financial return analysis, for example the costs of waste water purification. The question concerned has been included here in order to establish whether unexpected significant changes in licences or levies might occur.

In selecting the key aspects possible future societal developments should be taken into account in order to be able to anticipate hurdles or unexpected future applications. For some aspects this can be of such crucial importance that a technology forecasting analysis has to be drawn up. (In most cases the latter can also be used to assess non-technological developments.) Such a picture of the future may lead to the discovery of key aspects that would otherwise have been overlooked. By the end of Step 2 a number of aspects will have been selected which – due to their social or economic impact – are decisive in the possible realization of the project.

Step 3

Having selected the key aspects, the next step is to identify what groups, individuals or organizations will be helped or harmed by the new technology. The non-economic 'interests' should be included as well, for example, surface water life (whether it exists or not in a certain region), a breeding place for birds, a particular landscape, etc. For every 'interest' a list is made of the advantages or disadvantages compared with the existing situation. If the introduction of a new technology implies that an old technology will become obsolete the benefits of its elimination (advantages for the environment or for the consumer, because of a lower price), as well as the adverse effects (loss of jobs, for example), should be taken into account. Firstly, interested parties are those parties which have an interest in the production (personnel, financiers, suppliers, etc.) and the distributors, consumers and

Table 4.5 Power balance

1. What government policy supported, stimulated or permitted the development and introduction of the new technology (to be answered with respect to national, provincial or state, and municipal authorities; sometimes with respect to the European Commission)? Which policies does the new technology conflict with?
2. What commercial policy is the development in agreement with; what policy points does it conflict with?
3. Which organizations will control the technology in the development stage and in the production stage?
4. Which government organizations will be involved in the development, introduction and production stages of the new technology?
5. What will be the attitude of the trade unions toward the new technology? What will be the attitude of the works councils of the firms involved?
6. Can militant action groups be expected to protest against the introduction of the new technology? If so, why?
7. How will the new technology be received by the press and by consumer organizations?

8. Is there a chance of one or more political parties or politicians expressing an opinion for or against the new technology?

9. What persons, organizations, government departments, branches of trade and industry, etc. will the new technology provide with more work and influence?

10. What persons, organizations, government departments, branches of trade and industry will the new technology deprive of work and/or influence (for example, due to a gradual decrease in their influence over an older type of technology)?

11. Does any industrial firm, other than the one for which the study is being carried out, play a decisive role with respect to the new technology (for example, because there is a complete dependence on this industrial firm for the supply of a raw material or of a certain part)?

12. Is the new technology applicable to a new type of industrial organization in which employees bear a greater responsibility with respect to their own work and/or the functioning of the factory as a whole?

Table 4.6 Other aspects

1. Is it necessary to remain in a certain location because of the availability of raw materials, the production process, the market outlet, inflows or outflows of energy and materials, personnel, etc.?

2. Is it necessary to use one specific type of transport for the supply of raw materials and ancillary materials or for the conveyance of the finished product?

3. Is there any possibility that the product might increase or decrease the rate of growth of the population?

4. Does the new product contribute to cultural changes? Does it provoke objections on ethical or religious grounds?

5. Is land which is in some way irreplaceable or scarce (in an ecological sense, because of its historical significance, etc.) being used for this purpose? What are the alternatives?

6. Does the new technology have a detrimental effect on the landscape? Are problems anticipated in the future (expansion plans, construction of roads, waterways, airports, etc)? What are the alternatives?

7. Can the product or process reinforce or alter differences in income, faith or creed, age, colour, education, urbanization, etc.? Are problems to be expected in this respect? What are the alternatives?

8. Does the noise constitute a nuisance in the vicinity of the (future) factory? What norms are applicable or can be expected? How much would it cost to reduce the noise level to one-fifth the present volume?

9. What would be the extra burden imposed on the environment by:
   putting the factory into operation; terminating the operation
   cleaning and maintenance of the factory
   calamities?

10. What is the attitude of the people living in the vicinity?

11. Is there a possibility of government assistance in financing the special facilities for protection of the environment, supply of water, equipment to restrict the noise level, safety measures, etc., by offering investment deductions, increased write-offs, investment interest subsidies, or financial guarantees? Do these possibilities also exist for follow-on investments?

12. Does the product, the production process or the manufacturer have a negative image with respect to the environment? What kind of image does the competition have?

13. Is improper use of the product or improper discharge of waste flows dangerous? Is improper use to be expected? If so, what measures must be taken?

14 Can the technology be produced or consumed in other countries? Does use in other countries necessitate special requirements with respect to the production process or the product?

15. Is the product made from raw materials that come from developing countries?

16. Are patents belonging to other parties expected to present obstacles? If so, in which countries are these patents valid and when do they expire? If manufacturing were to take place in countries other than the one where it was initially intended, would this remove these obstacles?

17. Are the purpose and advantages of the new technology comprehensible to the consumers, the government and the public? If not, how can this be remedied?

Table 4.7 Factors that are eliminated or become superfluous

1. If the new technology is introduced, which facilities for production, repair and maintenance will become obsolete?
2. How much and what kind of unemployment will result?
3. What kind of capital will become worthless; how much and whose?
4. How much land is lost as a result of the new product's being produced, transported/stored and consumed? Sum up the adverse effects on the environment.
5. Whose power and influence is reduced due to the old technology's becoming obsolete? Whose know-how becomes obsolete?
6. List all the persons or groups whose incomes are reduced or whose work becomes less interesting or requires less responsibility as a result of introducing the new technology.

possibly the municipality where the production facilities are situated.

By the end of Steps 2 and 3 two lists of key aspects will have been drawn up, aspects representing the decisive benefits and adverse effects, viewed from every possible angle of present and future societal interest. Moreover, a list of parties to be affected either beneficially or adversely by the new technology has been drawn up.

Step 4

Using these two lists Step 4 examines modifications of the new technology or alternative technologies in such a way that its advantages are retained, or preferably enlarged and its disadvantages reduced. This can be done in the following way. First, with the help of Table 4.8, alternatives or variants of the new technology can be traced. An alternative may be to use another material for the production of the product, or to use another production technique. This should not be limited to the products and techniques for which the company has the know-how available. Suppose an aluminium processing industry comes to the conclusion that a certain product can be made much better with a carbon-fibre-intensified polyester. To invest in the aluminium variant would be short-sighted and co-operation with a manufacturer of artificial materials, disposing of the relevant know-how, would be an option.

Likewise, the search for variants should not be limited to the potentialities of the home company. A variant in this connection is meant to be a solution that keeps the basic principle of the technology intact – this in contradiction to the previously-mentioned term alternative – but whose component parts differ from the solution initially opted for.

When the number of alternatives and variants have been identified they can be checked against the previously-mentioned key aspects and the parties affected, either beneficially or adversely. This results in a so-called aspect-matrix. It has been drawn up by way of an example in Table 4.9. The key aspects mentioned here are:

- availability of manpower and know-how for a certain type of tanker-cleaning;
- discharge of a given substance polluting the environment; fire danger when using material *Y* (the extra costs of the insurance premium are included in the financial return analysis, but apparently the risk is so great that it returns here as an insuperable key aspect);
- the import of certain raw materials from the politically delicate country *Z*.

In this example four alternatives or variants have been identified which have been checked against the key aspects. Next, the risk of each alternative on every key aspect has been weighed as in a consumer's guide. This may seem a somewhat simple solution, but experience with the method in commercial life has shown that this way gives a brief and communicative summary of the results of technology assessment, on the basis of which clear decisions can be made.

Step 5

Once the project has been assessed concerning its societal risk, and optimized with the help of Step 4, it is advisable to trace what hidden societal risks there may be with suppliers or consumers. For it often happens that an investment with a completely acceptable societal risk fails because of social problems – with the supplier of raw materials or because the product of the investment is processed into a consumer commodity that is subsequently banned for quite a different reason – dragging the product down in its fall.

The analysis concerning the third investment criterion should not be confined to the company's own product alone, therefore. It is not only a matter of the so-called process column (the chain of mutually supplying companies) but also of processing waste material and suchlike. When these matters are included in the process column the so-called process column outline will be the result; in Figure 4.1 an example of a building project is given.

In Step 5 of a technology assessment, a process column outline such as this is drawn up first and then it is decided

Table 4.8 Alternatives

1. What need on the part of society does the new technology primarily aim to fulfil? How is this need measured? Is there a general consensus of opinion in government circles and among the public as to the seriousness of this need?

2. What are the most important short- and long-range positive and negative side-effects of the introduction of the new technology?

3. In what other ways can the above-mentioned need be met? In other words, what alternatives are there for the technology? Why was this particular technology selected?

4. What alternatives are there for the production process? Why was this particular process selected? How much flexibility does this process offer in meeting the stricter environmental and safety regulations? How flexible is the process with respect to the use of other raw materials, other qualities of water, other energy norms?

5. What modifications are possible within the selected technology? In other words, which modifications reduce:
   discharge of materials which pollute the environment?
   transport and storage of dangerous materials?
   consumption of energy?
   use of water?
   the quantity of (scarce) raw materials and ancillary materials?

6. Why have these particular modifications been chosen? How much flexibility is there to switch to other modifications at a later stage?

7. Do other firms have new processes or products which are designed to reduce the above-mentioned modifications and, if so, can they be incorporated into the project in question?

which stages in the outline then have to be analysed with the help of the technology assessment method (Steps 1-3 in this section). In situations where the influence of the project on suppliers and purchasers is very limited a shortened version of Step 5 will suffice.

Table 4.9 Example: aspect matrix

	Alternative			
Key aspects	*I*	*II*	*III*	*IV*
Availability of know-how on tanker-cleaning	–	++	+	–
Discharge of *X*	O	––	O	+
Fire danger *Y*	––	–	–	O
Imports from *Z*	––	++	+	+

Key: –– prohibitive
– unfavourable
O acceptable
+ attractive
++ no risks

Step 6

In this conclusive step the results are summarized and communicated in a clear and concise way. During the previous steps the opinions of the parties involved and of special advisers will have been expressed. These people should be able to find their own opinions reflected in the final report and to see what influence they actually had. The report should be geared to those people who want to be informed about the matter–those involved and the decision-makers–whereas the results should also be accessible to other members of the profession in order that they can evaluate them. If it is a large technology that is the subject of the study it is probable that more than one form of report will be drawn up, for example an extensive scientific report and summaries of methods and conclusions for those involved and for the decision-makers.

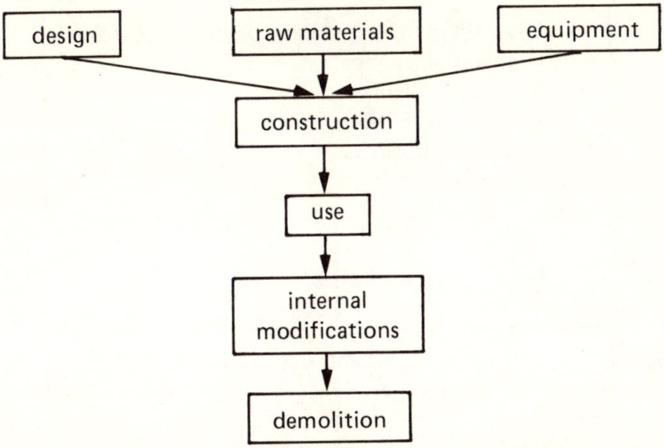

Figure 4.1 Example of a process column scheme for a building project

It is very difficult to maintain scientific objectivity while writing the report. During the study itself, the researchers may develop their own personal opinion as to the most desirable decision. Although there is no need to keep their opinion a secret, they do have to let the proper decision-making bodies make the decision, and not unconsciously try to influence them. The whole success of technology assessment depends on the willingness of the researchers to uphold their objectivity during the course of their work and to leave decisions to the decision-making authorities.

Summary and evaluation

With the help of technology assessment possible societal hurdles can be forecast, which may influence the investment project while it is in progress: the information gathered can also be used for the optimization of the project. The enterprise can check with the method described in this chapter to what extent the project comes up to the third investment criterion: the societal interest criterion. The method has been visualized in Figure 4.2: the main attention is focused on the aspect-matrix of Step 4.

Technology assessment is still in its infancy, few organizations make use of it, let alone use it systematically. In part

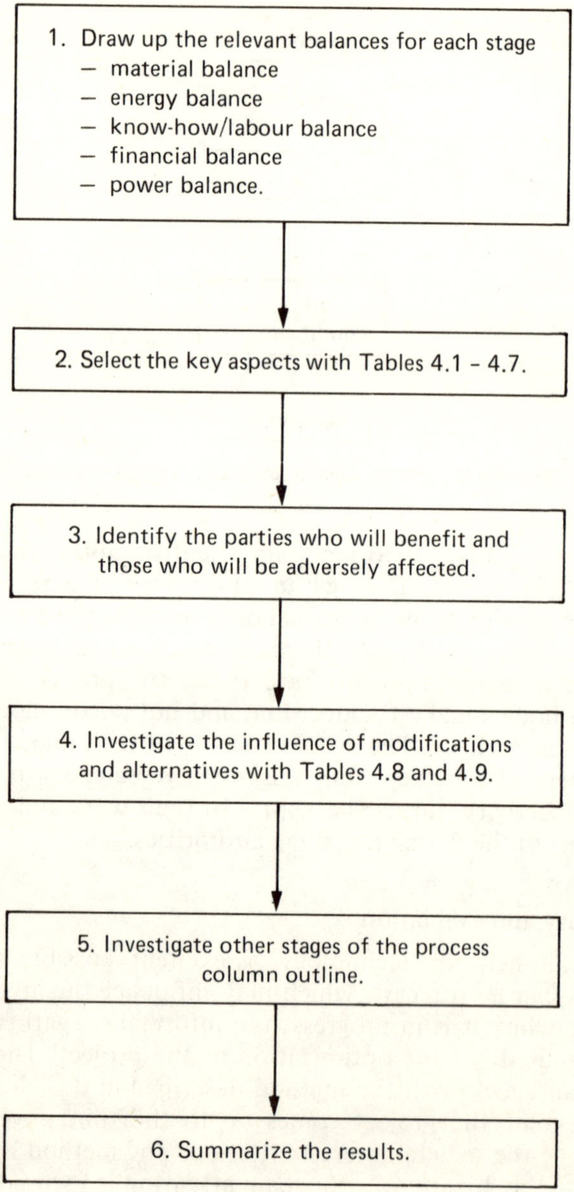

Figure 4.2 Steps in the concise technology assessment method

this is attributable to ignorance of the method and the line of thought preceding it, partly to the fear that tracing possible societal hurdles will hamper or block investments and especially the development of new products ('there is no smoke without fire'). In practice, people do take environmental and scarcity aspects into account, and also societal aspects, although not in a systematic way. This practice of half playing the ostrich is in strange contrast to the use of the finely-tuned methods of financial return analysis. This author expects and hopes, both for societal and business economic reasons, that technology assessment is going to become one of the standard management techniques.

5. WINDING UP

In this chapter a number of new subjects will be added to the material in the previous chapters. They concern, first, a shortened procedure for investment analysis. This procedure has been developed at the request of a number of companies, especially smaller ones in which systematic investment analysis is not yet common pratice.

This is followed in the second section by a short manual on the preparation of a feasibility study, that is a report in which all relevant aspects of an investment proposal are collected. Feasibility studies are the vehicle of communication between those concerned with investment selection; the results of the investment analysis as outlined before are an integral part of those studies.

Finally, in the third section we come back to the strategic and tactical trajectories as outlined in the first section. The role of systematic investment selection will be seen as a bridge between these two lines of thinking.

The third section terminates the desription of our method for investment analysis. In addition, Chapter 6 will deal with investment analysis in practice, with the annexes giving worked examples and an extension of the financial return analysis.

A shortened procedure

In Chapters 2 to 4 mention is made of possible limitations and simplifications of the methods presented. For the sake of improved accessibility a shortened method will be described below in which all the simplifications will be incorporated. This is the shortest way possible! However, the reader should be warned that this procedure is nothing more than a rather superficial analysis. Nevertheless, the method does have operational value and may be the starting point for a broader analysis.

Criterion I: financial return

Use the form of Table 5.1. This has been derived from Table 2.8 and uses the same symbols.

Step 1.

Assess the annual gross sales (line *a*) and the annual costs (line *b*). Also include under costs the real research and development costs, if any.

Step 2.

Assess the required investments for each year (line *o*) and calculate the depreciations according to the instructions in Step 3b on page 34 (line *d*).

Step 3.

Calculate the pre-tax income (line *e*), the ROI-income (line *g*); in doing this a corporation tax amounting to 50 per cent was calculated with it. If the corporation tax is 40 per cent, then $g=0.6e$; if it is 30 per cent, then $g=0.7e$, etc. Next, calculate the cash flow *h*.

Step 4

Calculate the expansions of the working capital (line *p*), e.g. as a percentage of the gross sales. N.B. It is the expansions of the working capital that are at stake and not the capital itself. The working capital itself only appears the first time, because then there is an expansion from capital = nil.

Table 5.1 Shortened form for pay-back period

Quantity	Code	Year									
		1	2	3	4	5	6	7	8	9	10
Gross sales	a										
Costs	b										
Depreciation	$d = 0.20$										
Pre-tax income	$e = a-b-d$										
ROI-income	$g = 0.5e$										
Cash flow	$h = g+d$										
Investments in fixed assets	o										
Expansion working capital	p										
Investments	$q = o+p$										
Cash-flow investments	$s = h-q$										
Accumulated	$S = \Sigma s$										

Step 5.

Finally, calculate the investment (line *q*), the difference between cash flow and investments (line *s*) and the same accumulated. The latter amount will be obtained by adding up the *s* amounts.

Step 6.

It will appear that *S* is initially negative, because in the beginning the project requires investments and yields little or nothing. As more money flows in, *S* approaches zero and after that becomes positive. The year in which *S* is positive for the first time is the pay-back period. At that moment the project has paid itself back. The shorter this pay-back period, the more attractive the project is in principle, that is as a first indication.

Criterion II: strategy and synergy

Answer the questions in Table 5.2 by ticking the boxes under the applicable keyword on the right side of the table. The questions have been derived from the forms in Chapter 3, which can be used for reference, should the questions in Table 5.2 be obscure due to their brevity.

Have all questions been answered, preferably by a multi-functional group of employees (research, production, marketing, finance)? Then a simplified strategy/synergy profile has been obtained, giving an idea of the extent to which the project encompasses the work that the company is able and wishes to do.

Criterion III: societal acceptance

This criterion traces unexpected hurdles, before or after the project has been executed, hurdles such as those concerning scarcity, environment and safety, imminent technological substitutes or changing needs or attitudes on the part of the public, for other than economic reasons (culture, politics, etc.).

Table 5.2 Simplified strategy/synergy profile

Questions	According to the questions the project is:				
	Negative	Neutral	Positive	Appealing	Very Appealing
Does the project have an appeal for the company as a whole, e.g. as a springboard for further diversification, internationalization, strengthening strong points, co-operation potential, decreased sensitivity to business cycles, improvement of image, better utilization of the raw materials and subsidiary organizations of the company?					
Does the project enhance the competitive power of the PMC of which it forms a part?					
Does the project strengthen the marketing strategy and does it lead to a better utilization of the marketing department?					
Same question for production.					
Same question for R&D.					

Step 1.

Go through the check-lists in Tables 4.1 to 4.7 in Chapter 4 and trace possible hurdles in this way. List these hurdles in the key aspects column of Table 5.3. (This is similar to Table 4.9 in Chapter 4.)

Step 2.

Trace those who would be affected by the project, either adversely or beneficially, were the project to be carried out. List these by means of keywords in the key aspects column.

Step 3.

Try to find alternatives for or variants on the investment, in which case the list of hurdles and those affected will change. Give the alternatives and variants roman numerals. In Table 5.3 four alternatives are shown, but there may in fact be more or fewer than this.

Step 4.

Establish, by means of study, advice from inside or outside experts or experiments, what weight each key aspect should have in the various alternatives. In doing so, follow the code as shown in Table 5.3. See Table 4.9 as an example.

Step 5.

Select the best variant possible or the best alternative possible.

Step 6.

Assess whether this version is acceptable or not.

For an explanation of this the reader is referred to p. 100,

Table 5.3 Aspect matrix

Key aspects	Alternative *I*	*II*	*III*	*IV*
1				
2				
3				
4				
5				

Key: –– prohibitive
– unfavourable
O acceptable
+ attractive
++ no risks

though the steps in that section have been numbered differently.

Setting up a feasibility study

A feasibility study results in a report which includes all relevant information for an investment decision. Apart from giving a description of the project, it should provide the answers to two questions:

- is the project attactive to our company?
- is our company attractive to the project?

The first question will be answered by the method described in Chapters 2 to 4, using the three investment criteria. The second question requires some explanation. A project can perfectly suit our company's requirements, financially, strategically and in terms of synergy and societal acceptability, yet, this leaves open the question of just why our company should take on this project, from the project's point of view. Would the project not be happier in some other company, where the synergy is larger, the strategic fit is better, the financial return is higher? If this question is answered in the affirmative, it means that, should a competitor create a similar project, he would be in a better competitive position and we could lose the contest, despite the desirability of such a project for our company.

This argument does not really introduce a new investment criterion as the arguments are already included in the strategy/synergy profile. One could, however, draw up a profile such that a competitor would consider the project. This may require some imagination since not all the strategic considerations and synergistic aspects of the competitor may be known. But enough is usually known from the situation of the major competitors to attempt it. By comparing the profiles, one can assess or at least estimate the problems that may arise when competitors put up a similar investment.

Let us start with the descriptive part first, however. This can usually be stated in four chapters of the feasibility report, one general, one on technical and cost aspects, one on market and marketing aspects and one on the capacity required. (See Table 5.4 for the suggested list of contents of such a report.)

Table 5.4 Classification of feasibility study

Chapter	Title
1	Project description
2	Know-how and technical details
3	Commercial details
4	Required capacity
5	Financial return
6	Strategy/synergy profile
7	Societal aspects
8	Options for competitors
9	Summary, recommendations, consequences

The first chapter will contain a general description of the project: What is its nature, its purpose and how does it fit in with other business activities and available resources? Who originated the project, what is its status, how much money has already been spent on it? Does the company already have experience with projects of this nature or is it a 'first'?

The second chapter deals with a technical description of the project and an estimate of the costs involved. These include possible development costs, investments in fixed assets and working capital, and all operational costs except sales costs. Operational costs include the cost of raw materials, labour, energy and other utilities, maintenance, hired services, management, and so on.

In addition to these descriptions, the technological strategy should be outlined. What savings can be expected from learning effects and scale effects? What development pattern should be followed? What alternatives have been considered?

The third chapter deals with the marketing aspects. What market niche will the project be aiming at? The results of market investigations will be presented as well as – where applicable – an analysis of the norms, values and lifestyles of customers. Next, the competitive field should be described as well as international tariff barriers, if applicable. Questions about present marketing capabilities and those to be developed should be highlighted *vis-à-vis* the external market situation. This will give the basis for the recommended marketing strategy which in its turn will give the marketing and sales costs, including costs of stocking the finished product and the costs of distribution. As a marketing strategy includes a pricing policy, a sales price can be developed. With these data the market share, as it is likely to develop over the years, can be estimated. From the estimated market development the sales volume can then be computed and thence the gross sales. In practice, the development of market share, sales prices and gross sales from market data and marketing strategies is not as straightforward as described here, since many alternatives will have to be considered, making the process iterative. In the feasibility report chapter only the results and brief passages on discarded alternatives need to be described.

In Chapter 4 the required manpower is established: what number of staff will have to be recruited and/or take a refresher course or be retrained. It is also necessary to describe requirements for management and to indicate whether that capacity is available or will have to be recruited: there is no need for names at this stage. In this chapter the question of the financial demands of the project is raised, beside the demands made upon facilities such as drawing department, workshop, technical services, training department, etc. Again, there will be iterations between the material of the first four chapters before these can be written up. Next, in Chapters 5 to 7 an account is given of the financial return analysis, the strategy/synergy profile and the aspect matrix. This does not only comprise the results, but also the key input and the considerations used.

The connection between Chapters 1 to 4 and Chapters 5 to 7 is that the first chapters provide the material that is systematically summarized and evaluated in the latter. In addition, new data can be entered in Chapters 5 to 7 or reference can be made to annexes.

In Chapter 8 the position of competitors *vis-à-vis* the project can be evaluated, together with possible attacks and the defence (or counter-attacks).

Finally, a summary of the project and recommendations on how to execute it and the strategies to be followed after execution conclude the feasibility study, together with a summary of the resources required.

This description of a feasibility study is based on a fairly substantial industrial project. In other situations fewer details may be required, while certain parts may not be applicable. Smaller projects require fewer details than large-scale projects; otherwise there is a risk that project selection will prove more expensive than the project itself. But also, in brief project proposals not meriting the name feasibility study, it will be wise to stick to the above-mentioned classification. In doing so, few vital matters will be overlooked, whereas the uniform approach of the feasibility studies simplifies comparison.

Although it is the objective of a feasibility study to inform the decision-makers, it is a cardinal example of the communicative power referred to elsewhere in this book, which is the result of the work of a multi-functional group of people. In this way they do not only inform their superiors, but each other also, which is of equal importance: the report is not only an end but a means.

Investment analysis as the link between strategic and tactical thinking

It has been said at the beginning of this chapter that it makes sense to think on two levels within an organization – the strategic and the tactical level. There the thesis was advanced that systematic investment analysis is especially useful since it functions as a link between the two ways of thinking. With the knowledge that the reader has picked up since then this thesis can be clarified, which is a good way to conclude this chapter.

The thinking has been visualized in Figure 5.1, in which the development on the strategic trajectory has been outlined on the left side and the development on the tactical trajectory on the right. From a regular analysis, carried out by the organization into the field of outside competition, technology and technological developments, economy, social and societal

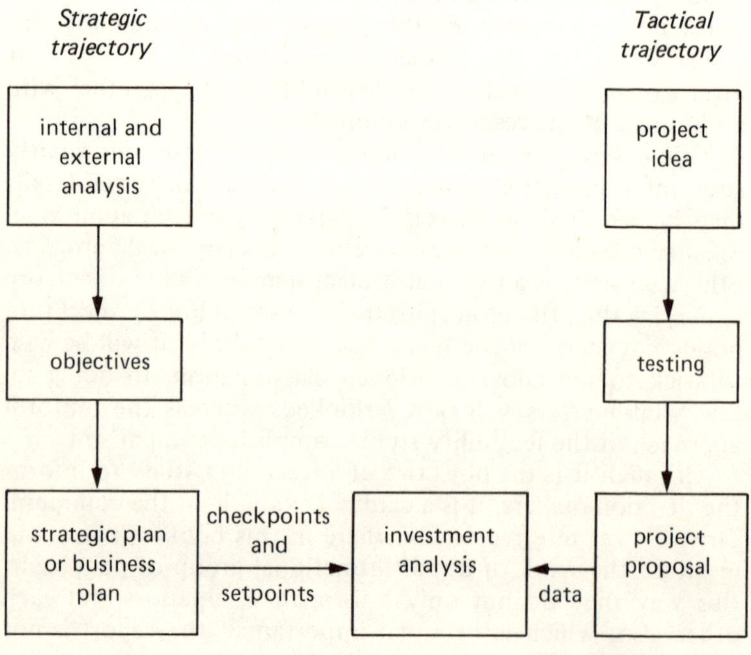

Figure 5.1 Investment analysis as the meeting point between strategy development and project development

developments, the organization selects the objectives that provide an optimal utilization of opportunities and challenges versus its own strong and weak points. This is laid down in a strategic plan, if the analysis is carried out for the entire company, or in a business plan if it is carried out occasionally for a particular PMC. These plans comprise an assessment of the company itself, which way it wants to go and what policy should be pursued to achieve it. It leads to checkpoints for the investment analysis: which financial demands are to be made, which questions to be asked with regard to the degree of synergy and affinity to strategy and which weights these answers should get, and in which way the broader societal responsibility is to be fulfilled.

The other trajectory sometimes starts with an idea, and anything and everything that precedes an idea: an intuition, irritation about something that goes wrong, a new market need or a technological potential manifesting itself. The idea is tested, it goes into further development, maybe it is constructed to scale or a pilot project is begun, and if the idea survives all these stages and is taking shape, a decision will then be necessary: to continue with it or to cease development. To this end a project proposal is drawn up, providing the details for the investment analysis. As we saw in the previous section, the results of this analysis together with the project proposal will be presented in the feasibility study.

With this diagram (Figure 5.1), which bypasses the fact that many project proposals are directly derived from the strategic plan, the link between both ways of thinking has been laid down and the intermediary role of the investment analysis clarified.

6 INVESTMENT SELECTION IN PRACTICE

During the preparatory stage of this book a number of students from the Graduate School of Management in Delft held interviews in about forty companies, including several banks. Although this was by no means systematic research it did yield information that supplemented the experience gathered by the author during his consultancy years and from the management seminars he participated in.

The picture of the use of systematic or methodical investment selection which emerges from this experience is far less sophisticated than one tends to think after having read the previous chapters. These are some examples from everyday life which speak for themselves without using the names of the relevant organizations.

A process industry

Process Industry, International, Turnover \$0.5m. Three types of investment are being distinguished, namely:

- Must investments. These are investments necessary to guarantee the company's continuity. Examples are the replacement of an old machine by a new one and investments in purification equipment to comply with obligations, arising from new laws.
- Depth investments. These are investments aimed at increasing the productivity of the existing capacity.
- Free investments. These investments are aimed at expanding capacity. Examples are: investing in a new laboratory and investments in new production processes. Free investments take up about 50 per cent of the total investments. The question of investment selection arises in particular in the case of depth and free investments.

The division manager can take an independent decision about investments up to $10,000, with a fixed annual maximum. Larger investments are judged by an investment steering committee. On this committee there are, among others, a member of the Board of Management, a technologist, and somebody from the financial department. This steering committee considers whether the investment fits in with the long-term strategy of the entire company and whether there are any synergistic effects. The steering committee traces which division wants to invest, what product is at stake and what the commercial interest is. Consequently, they decide where the investment should be made and what investment should take precedence. On the basis of these findings a priority list is drawn up by the steering committee. Only a limited number of these investments can be realized. This number is dependent, among other things, on the part of the available finances that is taken up by the must investments and the available manpower. The selected investments are laid down in a feasibility study. In this study an account is given of the means available for the investment, the equipment required, the position as regards competition, the payout time or the internal rate of return of the investment, and the costs of not effecting the investment.

Ideas for new investments come both from the top down and from the bottom up. The top draws up a long-term plan. From this plan a number of investments arise that are necessary for the plan to materialize (top down). An example of the bottom-up approach is the commerical department signalling a certain development, energy-conscious washing, for example, and asking the research department whether they can find something that links up with this development. If the research department succeeds an investment proposal is made.

Research costs are not converted into assets but considered as costs. The results of about half of research expenses are known to a certain extent; of the other half, the results are unknown. The research budget is fixed annually on the basis of projects, priorities, etc. The research is mainly carried out by the company itself and this internally generated know-how is thus a source of growth. Investment proposals are worked out by various different divisions.

The financial return on a project is assessed on the basis of the pay-back period. This applies in particular to free investments. The pay-back period has been fixed at three years. Investments which have a pay-back period of more than three years are rejected out of hand. This limitation has been chosen because technological developments move swiftly, so that investments pay off quickly and new investments can be made. In general there is no discounting of cash flows in calculating the pay-back period. This results from the fact that the extra capacity consequent upon the investment will in general be fully utilized from the beginning. Only in the case of increasing cash flows, when the extra capacity is not fully utilized from the beginning, does discounting take place.

The financial return on investments in energy-saving is assessed on the basis of the internal rate of return. This has to lie in between 30 and 35 per cent. The financial return of must investments is only assessed in the case of investments for the benefit of the environment. A check is made on whether it is better to pay the levies or to invest. The affinity of the investment to the long-term strategy and the degree of synergy are mainly established by the steering committee. The affinity to the long-term strategy is the main criterion for investment selection. The investment steering committee does not only trace whether the investment is synergistic to existing products and production processes, but also where the investment is to be made in order to get the highest degree of synergy. If the investment is to be made in a production process which requires great heat, for example, they will discover whether it is possible to carry out this process next to a heat-generating production plant.

An investment is considered to have passed the societal interest criterion when the government has issued a licence for the investment. Licences for new investments are only issued when the investment has a zero effect on the environment. Through the Chamber of Commerce organizations co-operate in fulfilling a licence policy.

A bank

This case considers an international bank in its function as credit supplier to investors. The bank distinguishes three types of investment:

- investments for short-term matters, such as financing working capital;
- investments for medium-term matters, such as a machine;
- investments for long-term matters, such as real estate.

The economic lifespan of the project is decisive and the objective is to attune the type of financing to it. In the examples it could be an (expansion of the) current account, a lease contract and a mortgage. This rule does not always apply. Sometimes financing is adapted to a high cash flow.

The investment idea always originates from the entrepreneur and he also takes the investment decision. If this leads to his applying for a credit the application has to be agreed minimally at two decision levels. Naturally, the entrepreneur can ask advice regarding his investment policy. However, the relationship between bank and entrepreneur is a voluntary one in which the entrepreneur's initiative will be decisive.

The process of investment selection by a bank progresses along the following lines: an entrepreneur submits an application for a credit to a local office. His client adviser looks into the application, paying attention to items like the general impression, the company's history, and the image of the company. The application is to be motivated by a number of data such as personal data and financial papers. Primarily, attention will be devoted to the credit side of the balance sheet, in particular the ratio between equity and invested capital, which should surpass certain acceptable standards. Postponed loans are included in the equity capital. There is no fixed standard, although the bank does not consider less than 20 per cent to be sound. For the retail trade this standard amounts to an average of 14 per cent.

Subsequently, the effect of the investment on this percentage is considered. The crucial question is whether the new ratio comes up to the standard or not. Apart from analysing the (change in) relative amount of the equity capital the bank also considers the increase in charges accompanying the investment, in particular repayments and interest payments. The company is seen as a black box yielding a certain cash flow. The minimum requirement is payment of interest and repayments: the so-called repayment potential. The quality of the management plays a prominent part in this.

So, in short, the decision about supplying a credit to a company depends on:

- The relative and absolute extent of the equity capital before and after the investment.
- The relative increase in charges and development of the trading results, in which an increase in the latter by means of an investment should minimally be able to bear payment of interest and repayments.
- The nature of the investment project, in particular the solidity of the prognosis. When the cash flows are very doubtful the bank prefers the company to be able to finance interest and repayments from current means. As a rule of thumb, the less solid the anticipated cash flow, the more the ability to cover costs from current means is taken into account.

Next, the client adviser gives his advice on the application for a credit on the basis of the above-mentioned considerations and the advice is sent with all other data to the decision-making body. In the event of it being approved the application will go one step higher for the final decision, so that every application gets approval from at least two decision-making levels. The application is seen to be even more trustworthy when it is accompanied by a chartered accountant's statement.

When this procedure is checked against the investment criteria described in this book a number of differences are noticeable which are largely accounted for by the bank's philosophy. According to this philosophy the third criterion is a subject for the entrepreneur. The bank does not make moral judgements and the only starting-point for societal acceptance is whether the investment is legal or not. It is only the financing of highly controversial matters (nuclear energy projects, for instance) that is avoided. For distortion of the image is to be prevented! Affinity to the company's strategy and possible synergistic effects also belong to the company. So it is the entrepreneur who puts together the entire policy of the company, which is based on five components:

the objective of the company;
the societal side-effects;
the investment capacity;
the human capacity;
the history of the company.

The company takes the initiative to invest in order to guarantee continuity or to improve the present situation. It is only when it is asked to that the bank will give advice concerning this purely entrepreneurial task. However, the bank looks over the entrepreneur's shoulder to keep track of his policy in a limited way.

A public works department

This case concerns a public works department with an annual level of investment of around $150m. From the contacts the department has with commercial life certain investment proposals emerge. These proposals are studied and further developed by the department. When they come up to certain specified requirements an application for a credit is drawn up which is then submitted to the city council.

When the project is being investigated the main consideration is the return on investment. This return is obtained by discounting the cash flows to be expected from the project with the interest that has to be paid on the credit granted; this is the weighted average of all the loans outstanding with the municipality. Subsequently, the difference between the results of realizing or rejecting the project will be taken into account. In this way the various alternatives can be compared and assessed as well.

Apart from the financial return there are other factors to be considered in analysing the project, such as: employment, safety, environment and welfare. In the investment statement the aspect deserving most emphasis is indicated for each project.

Because the department takes these factors into account when analysing an investment, projects are sometimes carried out which have a pay-back period of twenty to twenty-five years. This would be an unacceptably long period for normal companies. As far as other investment criteria are concerned, the department does not intentionally consider the synergy that may exist between the various projects. Each project is considered separately, so a calculation is made as to how much extra the project will yield, compared with the situation where the project was not carried out. This means that the strong synergistic effects will be included in the calculation. The department does not have a clear strategy of its own: few internal ideas will be generated, outside ideas from the commercial world are sought. These ideas can in principle be realized, provided they are not in conflict with municipal policy, in terms of environment, employment and safety.

A transport company

This case concerns an international transport company with considerable investments in transport media, distribution centres and services. Investment proposals have to be presented on a Capital Investment Application Form, which contains the results of a feasibility study (and a financial statement in particular), an extended summary of the motivation for the project and the alternatives which have been rejected.

The Investment Application Form is sent to the Investment Committee, a permanent committee of primarily financial specialists and experienced managers. This committee may invite specialists, who may or may not have been involved in the preparation of the project. Sometimes the proposal is returned to its originators, sometimes it is sent to the Board for approval. In the case of large investments the committee can also send more than one alternative to the Board and let them make the choice.

The criteria used are mainly financial and affinity to marketing strategy. For the financial analysis, pay-back period, net present value and internal rate of return are used simultaneously, with the emphasis on a short pay-back period.

The marketing group carries out market investigations on a very regular basis. The company spends a relatively substantial sum on market studies. These studies are used to update a medium-term planning system. Within the company this is called a real-time planning system, as any alterations of plan are instantly inserted. Most investment proposals originate from a comparison between this planning and projected capacity. In addition, market investigations frequently yield ideas for new services, which are investigated thoroughly since competition is very heavy.

Investments, other than in fixed assests, follow the same procedure. Recently, a plan to improve the motivation of the personnel was approved. This plan was not motivated by a financial analysis but was the result of investigations among customers. There it was shown that a further improvement in the attitude of the personnel would have a significant though unquantifiable impact on sales and competitive power. At the same time, the personnel department toyed with similar ideas as part of a personnel development plan.

Conclusion

The foregoing examples, drawn mainly from large companies, advanced in the field of investment selection, may be summarized as follows:

> The financial return criterion is used in a quantitative and systematic way, including all three methods mentioned in Chapter 2 (pay-back, net present value, internal rate of return). The author's experience with smaller companies is that calculations surpassing the pay-back calculation without discounting are the exception. More often than not these calculations are made by an accountant or adviser.
>
> The strategy/synergy profile, or something similar to it, is not used anywhere yet; in fact the relation between investment and strategy/synergy is rarely approached in a systematic way. Organizations developing a strategy or

business planning check investment proposals against these plans, often very carefully. But they seldom use any systematic method in doing so.

The same applies to assessing the societal acceptability and societal risks. The minimal position taken up by all investors is that they work according to the rules and include environmental levies in the financial return analysis in which a keen calculation is made as to whether it is more profitable to make an environmental investment or to pay the levies. Some organizations do sometimes list possible threats, but rarely in a systematic way.

The results of the enquiry by interview among forty companies mentioned earlier is listed in Table 6.1. In this table various criteria or methods are listed in the left-hand column. This is plotted against an indication of the use of these criteria or methods. In the matrix the percentage of companies is listed in each location.

Table 6.1 Use of investment criteria and methods

	Usage by code			
Criterion or method	++	+	+/–	–
	%	%	%	%
Intuitive approach	38	–	24	38
Pay-back, NPV, IRR	76	12	12	–
Affinity to strategy	38	38	12	12
Synergy	–	25	25	50
Strategy/synergy profile method	–	12	–	88
Aspect matrix method	25	12	25	38
Standard forms	75	–	25	–

Key:
- ++ very much present, with great similarity to the methods of this book
- \+ available, with a certain similarity to the methods of this book
- +/– depends on the nature of the investment
- – not available

It should be emphasized that the data in Table 6.1 are only an indication of the use of investment criteria and methods in a small and not necessarily representative sample of companies. These results confirm the conclusions stated earlier.

In conclusion we can say that there is much room for improvement in methods of investment selection. With respect to this, however, the author adopts an optimistic attitude. The widespread use of personal computers will enable many entrepreneurs and managers to 'play' with financial return analysis themselves. Strategic thinking finds its way to all levels of society. After initial violent clashes between eco-activists and commercial life in the late 1960s and early 1970s, a new generation of managers is developing, who deal with ecological and scarcity problems in a rational way, rational in the sense of the broad responsibility discussed in Chapter 4. It is for these reasons that one can expect that methods of systematic investment analysis will gradually find their way to becoming standard business practice.

ANNEXE 1: OMMEN LTD

This case describes a fictitious company which considers an equally fictitious investment project. First, general information about the company will be given. Next, the investment project will be described. A number of questions will have to be answered, using the methods described in Chapters 2 to 5. A detailed answer to these questions will terminate this annexe.

General description of Ommen Ltd

The chemical industry Ommen Ltd specializes in the development, manufacture and sale of vitamins, hormones and enzymes. In addition, there are a number of traded products. The majority of sales are realized in Western Europe and Latin America. For this market Ommen Ltd fully owns a production unit in Niteroi, Brazil, with about one hundred employees. The other 1,100 employees work at the main office in the Netherlands or at various overseas sales offices. Last year, the company's sales amounted to $181m. Four per cent of this sum was spent on research and development (R&D). Profit after tax was $1.6m.

History

Ommen Ltd was established in 1932 by the enterprising young chemist J.A. Haverkamp. After a number of years of tedious experimentation he found success with a new production process for making vitamins. Starting with licences, he managed to simplify the production process in such a way that several reductions in cost could be made. He established a small plant which became quite successful despite the economic depression.

The success of the company was to a great extent due to the activities of Mr W. Petersen, the main representative in the Netherlands for a German cosmetics manufacturer. This firm went bankrupt in 1934 and Petersen, living in the same town as Haverkamp and still in full possession of his faculties, found in him a natural partner. While Haverkamp organized

Balance sheet for 31 December 1984

	$		$
Land	2,250	Share capital	15,000
Buildings	9,800	Retained earnings	24,000
Machines	30,000	Other reserves	5,500
Finished products in stock	15,000	Research fund	3,250
Raw materials in stock	5,000	General reserves	20,850
Debtors	25,000	Creditors	17,500
Other assets	1,500	Current liabilities	2,150
Shares	3,250	Private account of	
Cash and bank	450	Mr Haverkamp	4,000
	$92,250		$92,250

Profit and loss account

	$	$
Sales		180,500,000
Raw materials	73,600,000	
Wages and social costs	96,500,000	
		170,100,000
Gross result		10,400,000
Depreciations		6,200,000
Net result		4,200,000
Extra depreciation Niteroi		1,000,000
Income before tax		3,200,000
Corporation tax (50%)		1,600,000
Net income		1,600,000

the patents and began production, Petersen created a sales network in Germany and the Netherlands and established what were to become well-known brand names.

At the onset of World War II Ommen Ltd was a steadily growing young enterprise. As there was a great scarcity of pharmaceuticals and hygiene products at this time Haverkamp and Petersen greatly expanded their product range. Raw materials were hard to come by and exports were impossible, but Ommen produced almost anything from aspirin to soap and they were regarded as a blessing by their customers.

When the war was over production of the 'war products' did not prove profitable and they were gradually discontinued. Ommen picked up its pre-war lines, concentrated on vitamins, and reconquered lost export markets. At the end of 1949 Petersen managed to negotiate contracts with major German and English chemist chains, and this more than doubled the turnover. Business flourished, but it took too much of Mr Petersen's energies, and he died in 1953 of a heart attack. Initially, Mr Haverkamp decided to go on without a commercial co-director, but he changed his mind when US investments in Europe soared in the late fifties and early sixties. He felt too old to cope with this new kind of competition and appointed Mr Teekens, a typical aggressive young marketing manager with an MBA from some obscure American University. Teekens had hardly begun work, when he modernized the product appearance and initiated exports to Latin America.

When sales were rising again Teekens launched the idea of 'diversification', about which he had read an article in *Long Range Planning*, and which had kept him awake a few nights. He claimed that Ommen needed 'a second leg' to stand on, with sales and profit potential approximating to those of the vitamins. His choice was hormone drugs, because he believed there was enormous potential for these, partly in view of the growing awareness of population problems, partly because of the explosion of Women's Lib. Market research confirmed what Teekens believed and Mr Haverkamp, being then fully occupied with his chance of a lifetime, a new, fully automated vitamin production plant, left him a free hand. Money was no problem and so R&D activities were started, led by

Dr. Rieske, whom Teekens had attracted as research manager. Unfortunately, results came too late and Teekens was forced to buy licences from an American company.

Mr Haverkamp showed little interest in the hormone activities and when his new vitamin plant was working well he gradually lost interest in the company. Teekens convinced him that life had more to offer than work and after deliberations with his family Mr Haverkamp decided to retire as Managing Director to become Chairman of the Supervisory Board. (Note: this is comparable to the non-executive Chairman of the Board in countries with a one-board system). Teekens then became MD and, instead of appointing a technical co-director, he attracted a young production engineer to become plant manager. He also managed to acquire a loyal sales manager and a manager for economic and social affairs, all reporting to him. Having been less than ten years in the company, Mr Teekens was fully in charge and was in possession of 20 per cent of the shares.

The hormone project was not very successful. Ommen came with little proprietary know-how and the best starting positions were already taken. Production synergy of hormones with vitamins was virtually non-existent, and synergy with marketing was also minimal. Although Ommen had invested heavily in hormone research, the position was not very strong.

The hormone research had an important side-effect, however, since a good research team was created and for one reason or another this team started work on enzymes at a time when this was hardly seen as a market option. These activities were adequately followed up by marketing activities, with the result that Ommen became a first-to-market company in a fancy business niche. Ommen took full advantage of the enzyme boom and still maintained an attractive position when the market for enzyme washing powder deteriorated.

The success of the enzymes brought back the spirit of the pre-hormone growth years and greatly strengthened Mr Teekens's position. He was regarded as a kind of wizard but he let Dr Rieske's R&D department share in the glory. Rieske could get as much money as he asked for and became a part-time

time professor of chemistry. Many new products were developed in his department but none of them became a commercial success. In fact there was not much need for new products since, with the newly started trading activities, the company had not two but four legs to stand on and business boomed.

In order to serve the Latin American market better, a plant was opened in Niteroi, Brazil in 1972 for the production of hormones and enzymes. In the same year Mr Haverkamp, now 70 years old, retired from the Board. Mr Teekens became especially active in the overseas marketing activities and the Niteroi operation, which he regarded as his baby. Despite his efforts it was not much of a success. There were heavy pre-operating losses and delays in getting production started. These costs reached their height in the oil crisis year 1973 and in 1974, for the first time in its history, Ommen made a loss. Fortunately, the market recovered and, following an efficiency programme, Ommen was out of the red again. However, profit margins were much lower than they had been, and attempts at further diversifications and internationalization all failed.

During the late seventies and early eighties Ommen came close to bankruptcy, but recovered each time by using tough efficiency drives, which reduced the workforce by more than one-third. In this way the company managed to beat inflation until the economic outlook improved in 1983 and signals for widening markets appeared.

Mr Teekens, now in his fifties, decided to make another attempt at diversification, but now in a much more selective way than before. First, the Brazilian plant was sold. Although it no longer made losses, it had never brought in much money and Ommen's position in hormones was considered hopeless. This meant that the European activities in hormones were terminated as well; in this way Ommen buried a dream.

A meeting with top management was called and they formulated the following objectives for the period 1984-89:

- Consolidation of positions in vitamins and enzymes, by further cost reductions in production, and careful product adaptations when the market requires it, both in outlook and in composition.

- Careful expansion of these products as export products to new overseas markets. Only when a 20 per cent market share is obtained should a proprietary marketing organization be considered. Only when sales through proprietary organizations in a particular area have been well above the original plan, capable of realizing all scale effects, should local production be considered.
- Careful diversification into new products with much synergy in either marketing or production, but preferably in both. These new products should complement vitamins or enzymes; totally new products should only be considered when there is a number of years' experience with them as traded products.
- Research activities should support the foregoing objectives with much more stringent project selection and budget control schemes. In production, the objective is to raise output levels and provide challenges for personnel, for instance by introducing quality control circles and careful experiments with new forms of industrial democracy. For managers, new challenges will have to be sought, while a systematic management development scheme will be initiated.

This four-point programme was widely discussed in Ommen and it met with equally wide approval. After the good years of the post-war boom, when everything seemed possible and substantial mistakes could easily be absorbed, after the messy and painful years of depression, when so many people had to leave and so many ideas had to be abandoned as unrealistic, the company regained new confidence with its no-nonsense, careful, selective and imaginative approach to its future.

Project description

In the above description we mentioned the significant research effort of Ommen Ltd in the enzyme area. Recently, one of the research workers, who had just paid a considerable dentist's bill for his family despite intensive use of fluoride toothpaste, suggested that it should be possible to make an enzyme toothpaste.

This idea was explored, and in a pilot investigation an enzyme was developed which was able to break down sugar and various other compounds that nurture the bacteria which cause caries. Its application to toothpaste was demonstrated to be possible and early reactions from dentists were very enthusiastic. The product still needs a fair amount of applied research as well as development work to fulfil health legislation requirements. Whether a fully approved product will result is still uncertain.

The enzyme developed can be used in two ways, first in toothpaste, second in a mouth-rinsing agent. If the latter is used after meals, it is sufficient to brush teeth only once a day.

Market research indicates that 500,000 tubes of toothpaste could be sold at a price of $6.00 in the shops. It is advised that these levels be maintained for three years and that then the price be reduced to $5.00; this would bring sales to million tubes in that year. This number can then be raised by 200,000 tubes per year. The trade margin is always 30 per cent of the retail price; the operational costs per tube are invariably $2.00. With the mouth rinse one has to be more cautious. Sales are estimated invariably at 200,00 units per year at a sales price of $7.00 with 30 per cent trade margin and operational costs of $2.00 per unit. The project can be completed by the R&D department in one year. This will cost $500,000, with a likelihood of success of 70 per cent. However, the department has already spent a substantial amount of money on the project; they wish to charge a symbolic amount of $100,000 to the project, which can be entered in the first year without taking into account its chances of success. Furthermore, after completion of this research work, the research department will have to spend $200,000 each year on supporting activities. All these costs will not be converted into assets. The likelihood of success of these supporting activities in the first two years is 0.8 and 0.9 respectively.

Following the research year engineering costs will be incurred over the next two years. These amount to $200,000. They will be turned into assets and will have to be divided by the success factors of 0.8 and 0.9 respectively. They can be depreciated in five years, depreciations starting in the year after the investment has been made.

All this means that production cannot start till the fourth year. This requires an investment in fixed assets of $2m in year 3, to be depreciated in five years. An extra investment of $1m is required in the year preceding the doubling of sales. This investment should also be depreciated in five years. The working capital required is estimated at 20 per cent of the sales-off-works, that is the turnover minus the trade margin. Corporation tax is 50 per cent. The project can benefit from government investment premiums of 25 per cent of fixed assets. These premiums have to be regarded as extra, tax-free income, to be added to line *g* of the finance return form. This ensures that the full depreciations can be deducted from the gross income in later years.

With respect to synergistic and strategic considerations, it should be noted that the expectations for the mouth-rinsing agent have been kept intentionally low. This product will be entirely new to households, which makes its commercial success rather unpredictable. However, there are indications that this product could be a big hit, and this factor has not been included in the above data. Schools have already agreed to buy a rinsing agent for after-lunch use. There are also refectories willing to sell the product as a regular service.

In the R&D department it is felt that more effective enzymes could yet be developed. The marketing department will set up a big campaign, using the same brand name as for the vitamins.

Exercise

Using the above data, common sense and, where necessary, some imagination, try to estimate the following. Use the financial return analysis in Chapter 2 and the short strategy/synergy and societal aspects methods in Chapter 5.

- the financial return (i.e. the pay-back period, discounted pay-back period and net present value at 8 per cent discount rate and the internal rate of return);
- the synergy and affinity to strategy;
- the societal acceptability and risk.

1. *Suggested solution: financial return*

The results of the analysis are presented in Table A1.2.

1.a *Research costs*

These are 500 in year 1, with a likelihood of success of 0.7 (lines *b* and *c*). As the old research costs of 100 do not have to be divided by a success factor, they can be entered as other costs in line b_1. Research costs in all other years are 200; in years 2 and 3 the success factors are 0.8 and 0.9 respectively, after that they are equal to1.

The engineering costs are 200 for years 2 and 3, with success factors 0.8 and 0.9.

From the data on research and engineering it can be deduced that production and sales start in year 4.

1.b *Investments in fixed assets*

These are 2,000 in year 3 and 1,000 in year 6 because production and sales double in year 7. The depreciation can then be found from Table A1.1.

Table A1.1 Depreciation

Amount (year)	3	4	5	6	7	8	9	10
250 (2)	50	50	50	50	50	–	–	–
220 (3)	–	44	44	44	44	44	–	–
2,000 (3)	–	400	400	400	400	400	–	–
1,000 (6)	–	–	–	–	200	200	200	200
Total (line *d*)	50	494	494	494	649	644	200	200

The investment premiums of 500 in year 3 and 250 in year 6 can be entered in line *g*, as indicated in the project description.

1.c *Sales*

For the sales in line *a* the sales minus trade margin will be used as these are the basis for the computation of the working capital.

Sales for the rinsing agent are invariably 200,000 X 7 X 70% = 980 per year, starting year 4.
For the toothpaste, sales for years 4, 5 and 6 are: 500,00 X 6 X 70% = 2,100. Total sales in these years are therefore 2,100 + 980 = 3,080. For the following years, the sales are:

year 7 : 1m X 5 X 70% = 3,500 + 980 = 4,480
year 8 : 1.2m X 5 X 70% = 4,200 + 980 = 5,180
year 9 : 1.4m X 5 X 70% = 4,900 + 980 = 5,880
year 10 : 1.6m X 5 X 70% = 5,600 + 980 = 6,580.

The working capital is 20 per cent of the sales; the extensions of working capital can then readily be computed. After this, line *q* can be computed.

1.d *Costs*

Production costs for the rinsing agent are invariably 200,00 X 2 = 400 per year. Those for the toothpaste are 500,000 X 2 = 1,000 in years 4, 5 and 6; this leads to total costs of 1,400 in these years. For the following years, these are:

year 7 : 1m X 2 = 2,000 + 400 = 2,400
year 8 : 1.2m X 2 = 2,400 + 400 = 2,800
year 9 : 1.4m X 2 = 2,800 + 400 = 3,200
year 10 : 1.6m X 2 = 3,200 + 400 = 3,600.

Filling these costs in on line *b* allows the computation of line *h* to be completed.

1.e *Financial criteria*

From *h* and *q*, *s* and *S* can be computed. The accumulated cash flow *S* becomes positive after almost exactly seven years, or four years after the start of production.

Discounting by 8 per cent gives lines *u* and *U*. From the latter a discounted pay-back period of seven years and eight months can be derived, and a net present value of 1,462 ($1,462,000).

Calculation of the ROI shows rapidly expanding percentages, illustrating the relative uselessness of this criterion. When other discounting percentages are used, the following

Table A1.2 Result of Ommen Ltd project (in $1,000)

Quantity	*Code*	*Year*									
		1	*2*	*3*	*4*	*5*	*6*	*7*	*8*	*9*	*10*
Gross sales	a	–	–	–	3,080	3,080	3,080	4,480	5,180	5,880	6,580
Research costs	b	500	200	200	200	200	200	200	200	200	200
Likelihood of success	c	0.7	0.8	0.9	1	1	1	1	1	1	1
Fictional research costs	$b_1 = b/c$	714	250	222	200	200	200	200	200	200	200
Other costs	b_2	100	–	–	1,400	1,400	1,400	2,400	2,800	3,200	3,600
Depreciation	$d = 0.2(n+o)$	–	–	50	494	494	494	694	644	200	200
Income before tax	$e = a - b_1 - b_2 - d$	(814)	(250)	(272)	986	986	986	1,186	1,536	2,280	2,580
Tax	$f = 0.5\,e$	(407)	(125)	(136)	493	493	493	593	768	1,140	1,290
ROI-income	$g = e - f$	(407)	(125)	364	493	493	743	593	768	1,140	1,290
Cash flow	$h = g + d$	(407)	(125)	414	987	987	1,237	1,287	1,412	1,340	1,490
Research investment	k		200	200							
Likelihood of success	m		0.8	0.9							
Fictional research investment	$n = k/m$		250	222							

Investment fixed assets	o		–	2,000			1,000				
Expansion working capital	p		–	–	616	0	0	280	140	140	140
Investments	$q = n+o+p$	0	250	2,222	616	0	1,000	280	140	140	140
Cash-flow – investments	$s = h-q$	(407)	(375)	(1,808)	371	987	237	1,007	1,272	1,200	1,350
Same, accumulated	$S = \Sigma s$	(407)	(782)	(2,590)	(2,219)	(1,232)	(995)	12	1,284	2,484	3,834
Discounting factor	$t = (l+r)^i$	1.08	1.16	1.26	1.36	1.47	1.59	1.71	1.85	2.00	2.16
Discounted cash flow (DCF)	$u = s/t$	(377)	(323)	(1,435)	273	671	149	589	688	600	625
Net present value	$U = \Sigma u$	(377)	(700)	(2,134)	(1,861)	(1,189)	(1,040)	(451)	237	837	1,462
Accumulated investments	$Q = \Sigma q$			2,470	3,086	3,086	4,086	4,366	4,506	4,646	4,786
Accumulated depreciations	$D = \Sigma d$			50	544	1,038	1,532	2,226	2,870	3,070	3,270
Invested capital	$v = Q-D$			2,420	2,542	2,048	2,554	2,140	1,636	1,576	1,516
ROI	$w = g/v$			5	19	24	24	28	47	72	85

r = discount rate
i = year number

Note: capital symbols identify accumulated values. Negative amounts are in parenthesis. It is assumed that the corporation tax rate is 50% i.e. $f = 0.5e$

Table A1.3 Computer printout for Ommen Ltd with 8% discount rate

PROFIT AND LOSS ACCOUNT

Quantity	1	2	3	4	5	6	7	8	9	10
Gross sales	–	–	1,000	3,080	3,080	3,580	4,480	5,180	5,880	6,580
Research costs	500	200	200	200	200	200	200	200	200	200
Likelihood of success	70	80	90	100	100	100	100	100	100	100
Fictional R&DC	714	250	222	200	200	200	200	200	200	200
Other costs	100	–	–	1,400	1,400	1,400	2,400	2,800	3,200	3,600
Depreciation	–	–	50	494	494	494	694	644	200	200
Ebit.	-814	-250	728	986	986	1,486	1,186	1,536	2,280	2,580
Tax %	50	50	50	50	50	50	50	50	50	50
Tax	-407	-125	364	493	493	743	593	768	1,140	1,290
ROI-income	-407	-125	364	493	493	743	593	768	1,140	1,290
Int. paid	–	–	–	–	–	–	–	–	–	–
Tax rec.	–	–	–	–	–	–	–	–	–	–
Int. after	–	–	–	–	–	–	–	–	–	–
Net income	-407	-125	364	493	493	743	593	768	1,140	1,290

FINANCE PLAN

Quantity	1	2	3	4	5	6	7	8	9	10
Net income	-407	-125	364	493	493	743	593	768	1,140	1,290
Depreciation	–	–	50	494	494	494	694	644	200	200
Cash flow	-407	-125	414	987	987	1,237	1,287	1,412	1,340	1,490
Res. inv.	–	200	200	–	–	–	–	–	–	–
Likelihood of success	100	80	90	100	100	100	100	100	100	100
Fictional res.	–	250	222	–	–	–	–	–	–	–
Capital Expen.	–	–	2,000	–	–	1,000	–	–	–	–
Working capital	–	–	–	616	616	616	896	1,036	1,176	1,316
Exp. W.C.	–	–	–	616	–	–	280	140	140	140
Inv.	–	250	2,222	616	–	1,000	280	140	140	140
Diff.	-407	-375	-1,808	371	987	237	1,007	1,272	1,200	1,350

FINANCIAL RETURN ANALYSIS

Quantity	1	2	3	4	5	6	7	8	9	10
Cash flow	-407	-375	-1,808	371	987	237	1,007	1,272	1,200	1,350
Cum. cash flow	-407	-782	-2,590	-2,219	-1,232	-995	12	1,284	2,484	3,834
Work. cap.	–	–	–	616	616	616	896	1,036	1,176	1,316
F.A.	–	250	2,422	1,928	1,434	1,940	1,246	602	402	202
Liq. F.A.	–	25	242	193	143	194	125	60	40	20
Undisc. value	-407	-757	-2,348	-1,410	-473	-185	1,033	2,380	3,700	5,170
Discount (%)	8	8	8	8	8	8	8	8	8	8
Disc. fact.	1.08	1.1664	1.2597	1.3604	1.4693	1.5868	1.7138	1.8509	1.9990	2.1589
Disc. cash	-377	-322	-1,435	273	672	149	588	687	600	625
Cum. disc. cash	-377	-699	-2,134	-1,861	-1,189	-1,040	-452	235	835	1,460

Table A1.4 Printout for Ommen Ltd at 15%

FINANCIAL RETURN ANALYSIS

Quantity	1	2	3	4	5	6	7	8	9	10
Cash flow	-407	-375	-2,308	371	987	-13	1,007	1,272	1,200	1,350
Cum. cash flow	-407	-782	-3,090	-2,719	-1,732	-1,745	-738	534	1,734	3,084
Work. cap.	—	—	—	616	616	616	896	1,036	1,176	1,316
F.A.	—	250	2,422	1,928	1,434	1,940	1,246	602	402	202
Liq. F.A.	—	25	242	193	143	194	125	60	40	20
Undis. value	-407	-757	-2,848	-1,910	-973	-935	283	1,630	2,950	4,420
Discount %	15	15	15	15	15	15	15	15	15	15
Disc. factor	1.15	1.3225	1.5208	1.7490	2.0113	2.3130	2.6600	3.0590	3.5178	4.0455
Cum. disc. cash	-354	-284	-1,518	212	491	-6	379	416	341	334
Same account	-354	-638	-2,156	-1,944	-1,453	-1,459	-1,080	-664	-323	11

net present values result: 322 of 12 per cent and 11 for 15 per cent. The conclusion, therefore, is that the internal rate of return is approximately 15 per cent, which is very attractive. This is all the more so as the effects of the expansion in year 7 have not yet been fully taken into account.

The results for 8 per cent discount rate are given in Table A1.2. Table A1.3 gives the computer printout for this percentage and Table A1.4 gives the results for the discount rate 15 per cent, which is the internal rate of return.

2. *Strategy/synergy*

Next, the questions derived from Table 5.2 have to be answered, with reference to the questions on the questionnaires at the end of Chapter 3. The results are given in Table A1.5. Answering these questions comes down to checking the project against the four-point programme in the general description of Ommen Ltd; this is an illustration of the approach depicted in Figure 5.1.

It seems that the project fits well with the diversification strategy, as it is closely linked with the know-how and production capabilities as far as enzymes are concerned, while the marketing could go through the existing vitamin channels. The product could become a very big seller, especially the mouth-rinsing agent, although there are still many uncertainties. All this makes the project seem appealing with respect to the first question in Table 1.5; if the risks could be better assessed it may even be very appealing because, from the corporate point of view, this is exactly what is wanted.

The second question in Table A1.5 is not answered because the project would comprise a new PMC. The marketing question can be answered by 'appealing' and the product question by 'positive'; the utilization of the production facilities will undoubtedly improve (captive use of enzymes), but not to a great extent, and the required mixing and packaging facilities have very little to do with the facilities already available. For R&D the project can be labelled 'very appealing', as it represents a real breakthrough in enzyme technology which may have an important impact for the company in the future.

Table A1.5 Strategy/synergy profile for Ommen Ltd

Questions	According to the questions the project is:				
	Negative	Neutral	Positive	Appealing	Very appealing
Does the project have an appeal for the company as a whole, e.g. as a springboard for further diversification, internationalization, strengthening strong points, co-operation potential, decreasing sensitivity to market tendencies, improvement of image, better utilization of the raw materials and subsidiary organizations of the company?				●	
Does the project enhance the competitive power of the PMC of which it forms a part?					
Does the project strengthen the marketing strategy and does it lead to a better utilization of the marketing department?				●	
Same question for production.			●		
Same question for R&D.					●

This discussion terminates the strategy/synergy question. It should be noted that the foregoing are subjective judgements and as such they are not a mathematically perfect answer. Other analysts than the present author might give other judgements. There is only one way to assess whose pudding is best: by eating it.

3. Societal aspects

It is difficult to give a full aspects matrix in a book like this because it requires detailed technical and scientific knowledge as well as an awareness of legal and other aspects.

Aspects which require attention are:

- product safety;
- product behaviour during (over-long) storage in, e.g. retail shops, or storage at too high temperatures, etc.;
- possible allergic reactions from users of the toothpaste and production workers;
- attitudes of dentists, who may not like the product if it is successful in beating caries;
- environmental aspects;
- lifestyle aspects. Will people really care about their teeth in the long run?
- developments in sweeteners which might reduce the sugar component of the average diet, thus reducing the damage done by caries;
- competition will undoubtedly try to prove that the enzymes have no additional effect when compared to normal fluorized toothpastes.

This list could be extended. Some items may require the development of an alternative product (other enzymes), others need an extensive and objective scientific investigation of the effects of the product, followed by professional introductions to dentists, teachers, clinics and so on. Failure to do so in time might result in an initially negative appeal (dangerous, costly, unnecessary) which may be impossible to counteract after the product has been launched.

ANNEXE 2: DAIRADIANT INC.

Diaradiant Inc. is a medium-sized, Midwest US diary company which is owned by a group of cattle famers who supply the company with part of their milk production. Dairadiant increases the value of this raw material by turning it into a range of consumer items and intermediary products, such as condensed (concentrated) milk, various milk powders, puddings, yoghurts, and so on. The company has been quite innovative, especially in the area of coffee creamers for slot machines and desserts; the latter are supplied to restaurants and distributed via supermarkets. The company spends about 4 per cent of its sales on R&D, which is way above average in the food and beverage industry.

Recently, a new type of long-life yoghurt was developed for the top end of the consumer market, to be sold in health food shops. The project is out of the research phase, although it will still require attention from the R&D department. In 1985 costs of scaling-up alone will have to be made, estimated at $3m, with a likelihood of success of virtually 100 per cent. The project can use an old installation which would otherwise be useless after 1985. This installation costs $3m. In addition, an investment in fixed assets of $6m is required. The costs of scaling-up will be converted into assets; all investments will be depreciated in five years. The 1983 and 1984 depreciations of old installations have been covered by a previous project and so will the 1985 depreciation.

The R&D costs were $3.2m in 1983 and $1.6m in 1984. At the beginning of these two years the chances of success were estimated at 40 and 60 per cent respectively. These costs must be taken into account in the project analysis. In addition, from 1985 up to and including 1988, there will be annual research expenses of $2m. Not all research costs will be converted into assets.

Production and sales are scheduled to start on 1st January 1986. The company expects to sell 5m one-litre bottles in both 1986 and 1987. The selling price will be \$2.50, with production costs estimated at \$1.10 per bottle. Owing to the anticipated short lifecycle the number of bottles sold will decrease by 20 per cent per annum after 1987. In addition, a price decrease of 10 per cent per annum is regarded as necessary after 1st January 1987. As the farmers will require more money for their milk production costs will increase by 5 per cent per annum from 1st January 1986. As the company will have to finance both the farmers and the retailers a working capital of 50 per cent of the sales is required.

Exercise

Estimate the discounted pay-back period and the net present value after ten years at 8 per cent discount rate. Compute the internal rate of return. Comment on the synergistic, strategic and societal aspects and formulate advice for the Board of Governors about the execution of the project.

Suggested solution

First, make a financial analysis, using the method in Chapter 2. The results are listed in Table A2.2

Investments and depreciations

(a) scaling-up: \$3m in line *n*. Depreciate normally in five years;
(b) new fixed assets: \$6m in line *o*. Depreciate normally in five years;
(c) old fixed assets: \$3m. Three old depreciations of \$0.6m have already been charged to another project, so an investment of \$1.2m only remains, to be written off in two years (1986 and 1987).

Total investment in 1985 is hence \$10.2m. Depreciations are \$2.4m in 1986 and 1987; \$1.8m in 1988-90.

Research

Research costs from the past should be taken into account. As the project is already 100 per cent successful no risk factors should be applied; the appropriate information was superfluous. The costs will have to be discounted, however. This makes the old research costs, to be entered in line *b*, in 1985 equal to: $3.2 \times 1.08^2 + 1.6 \times 1.08 + 2 = \$7.46$m. For the years 1986 up to and including 1988, $2m should be entered in *b*.

Table A2.1 Sales and costs

Year	1986	1987	1988	1989	1990	1991	1992	1993	1994
Number of bottles	5.0	5.0	4.0	3.2	2.56	2.05	1.64	1.31	1.05
Sales price	2.5	2.5	2.25	2.03	1.83	1.64	1.48	1.33	1.20
Line *a*	12.5	12.5	9.0	6.50	4.68	3.36	2.43	1.74	1.26
Costs	1.1	1.16	1.21	1.27	1.34	1.40	1.47	1.55	1.63
Line b_2	5.5	5.8	4.84	4.06	3.43	2.87	2.41	2.03	1.71

Computation 1

The computation is presented in Table A2.2. This table shows some peculiar results. As could be expected from the narrowing margin between price and production costs, the cash flow decreases rapidly after the first two good years. In fact, in the years 1993 and 1994, the cash flow is even negative. In these years costs are higher than sales, meaning that the project would be terminated anyway at the end of 1992.

Owing to decreasing sales, the required working capital also decreases, giving negative working capital expansions after 1987. The calculation method assumes that stock levels can be maintained in proportion to sales. In practice this can be extremely difficult and many companies have got into trouble for not cutting down on working capital in time when sales figures came down.

Table A2.2 First computation for Dairadiant Inc.

Quantity	Code	Year									
		1985	1986	1987	1988	1989	1990	1991	1992	1993	1994
Gross sales	a	0	12.5	12.5	9	6.5	4.68	3.36	2.43	1.74	1.26
Research costs	b	7.46	2	2	2	0	0	0	0	0	0
Likelihood of success	c	1	1	1	1						
Fictional research costs	$b_1 = b/c$	7.46	2	2	2						
Other costs	b_2	0	5.5	5.8	4.84	4.06	3.43	2.87	2.41	2.03	1.71
Depreciation	$d = 0.2\,(n+o)$	0	2.4	2.4	1.8	1.8	1.8	–	–	–	–
Income before tax	$e = a-b_1-b_2-d$	(7.46)	2.6	2.3	0.36	0.64	(0.55)	0.49	0.02	(0.29)	(0.45)
Tax	$f = 0.5e$	(3.73)	1.3	1.2	0.18	0.32	(0.28)	0.25	0.01	(0.15)	(0.23)
ROI-income	$g = e-f$	(3.73)	1.3	1.1	0.18	0.32	(0.27)	0.24	0.01	(0.14)	(0.22)
Cash flow	$h = g+d$	(3.73)	3.7	3.5	1.98	2.12	1.53	0.24	0.01	(0.14)	(0.22)
Research investment	k										
Likelihood of success	m										
Fictional research investment	$n = k/m$	3									
Investment fixed assets	o	7.2									

Expansion working capital	p	0	6.25	0	(1.75)	(1.25)	(0.91)	(0.66)	(0.47)	(0.35)	(0.24)
Investments	$q = n+o+p$	10.2	6.25	0	(1.75)	(1.25)	(0.91)	(0.66)	(0.47)	(0.35)	(0.24)
Cash-flow - investments	$s = h-q$	(13.93)	(2.55)	3.5	3.73	3.37	2.44	0.90	0.48	0.21	0.02
Same, accumulated	$S = \Sigma s$	(13.93)	(16.48)	(12.98)	(9.25)	(5.88)	(3.44)	(2.54)	(2.06)	(1.85)	(1.83)
Discounting factor	$t = (l+r)^{i}$	1.08	1.16	1.26	1.36	1.47	1.59	1.71	1.85	2.00	2.16
Discounted cash flow (DCF)	$u = s/t$	(12.90)	(2.20)	2.78	2.74	2.29	1.53	0.53	0.26	0.11	0.01
Net present value	$U = \Sigma u$	(12.90)	(15.10)	(12.32)	(9.58)	(7.29)	(5.76)	(5.23)	(4.97)	(4.86)	(4.85)
Accumulated investments	$Q = \Sigma q$										
Accumulated depreciations	$D = \Sigma d$										
Invested capital	$v = Q-D$										
ROI	$w = g/v$										

r = discount rate
i = year number

Note: Capital symbols identify accumulated values. Negative amounts are in parentheses. It is assumed that the corporation tax rate is 50%.

The accumulated, undiscounted cash flow *s* stays negative throughout the ten years under consideration. If the project could be terminated at the end of 1992 and the remaining working capital fully recovered, the cash flow *S* would be (2.06) + 1.21 = (0.85) – still a negative figure. With *S* staying negative there is no sense in computing the net present value at a discount rate as this will only be more negative still. When the project is carried out it will cost the company money. However, if it is not carried out, it will also cost money as some expenses have already been incurred. These include the old research expenses of $5.46m and the old investment in fixed assets of $1.2m. If we leave these expenses out we get a better picture of the options of continuation or termination for the project.

Computation 2

Omitting these two items, the project can be recalculated and the results are given in Table A2.3. The undiscounted accumulated cash flow is now positive, the undiscounted pay-back period being five years and one month after commencement of production and sales. This is a rather long period.

When the negative cash flows *h* in the years 1993 and 1994 are not taken into account and when it is assumed that the working capital can be fully recovered when the project is terminated on 1 January 1993, then the internal rate of return is about 5 per cent. This is still not a good result as banks offer better rates than this. Financially speaking, the project is a disaster.

Further considerations

The above conclusion is based on the assumption that the data on which the calculation is based can be fully trusted. There are some question marks, however. Is it really necessary to spend $2m on research expenses for four whole years? If we put the average cost of a research worker at $50,000 per annum this comes down to a staff of forty on a fairly standard product which was all set after the scaling-up. Is the research department overstaffed and is the R&D manager trying to find accounts for his excess people? Is it logical to spend more than one-third of production costs on research? Or 16 per cent of sales? Even the electronics and pharmaceutical industries rarely reach such levels, if ever. It is difficult to argue with selling price and production costs, but is the lifecycle so short that such a drastic assumption of an annual decline of 20 per cent of sales has to be made?

In summary one gets the impression that the project has been 'computed (or better: assumed) down'. The Board would certainly have a closer look at these assumptions. If research costs could be got down to 10 per cent of what has been assumed, which would still leave four people employed, the project would then become quite healthy, as the reader can easily confirm.

A second consideration is that one does not decide by financial return alone. It appears from the text that the yoghurt and dessert activities are of a long-term nature, which one does not abandon because of one bad project. In addition: what are the social costs of trimming the sales, the research and the production departments? There may be some very good strategic reasons for the continuation of the project, and if this is so, the Board would have to redesign the project in such a way that it became financially attractive.

Table A2.3 Second computation for Dairadiant Inc.

Quantity	Code	Year									
		1985	1986	1987	1988	1989	1990	1991	1992	1993	1994
Gross sales	a	0	12.5	12.5	9	6.5	4.68	3.36	2.43		
Research costs	b	2	2	2	2						
Likelihood of success	c	1	1	1	1						
Fictional research costs	$b_1 = b/c$	2	2	2	2						
Other costs	b_2	–	5.5	5.8	4.84	4.06	3.43	2.87	2.41		
Depreciation	$d = 0.2\ (n+o)$	–	1.8	1.8	1.8	1.8	1.8				
Income before tax	$e = a-b_1-b_2-d$	(2)	3.2	2.9	0.36	0.64	(0.55)	0.49	0.02		
Tax	$f = 0.5e$	(1)	1.6	1.5	0.18	0.32	(0.28)	0.25	0.01		
ROI-income	$g = e-f$	(1)	1.6	1.4	0.18	0.32	(0.27)	0.24	0.01		
Cash flow	$h = g+d$	(1)	3.4	3.2	1.98	2.12	1.53	0.24	0.01		
Research investment	k										
Likelihood of success	m										
Fictional research investment	$n = k/m$	3									
Investment fixed assets	o	6									

Expansion working capital	p	0	6.25	0	(1.75)	(1.25)	(0.91)	(0.66)	(0.47)	(1.21)
Investments	$q = n+o+p$	9	6.25	0	(1.75)	(1.25)	(0.91)	(0.66)	(0.47)	(1.21)
Cash-flow - investments	$s = h-q$	(10)	(2.85)	3.2	3.73	3.37	2.44	0.90	0.48	1.21
Same, accumulated	$S = \Sigma s$	(10)	(12.85)	(9.65)	(5.92)	(2.55)	(0.11)	0.79	1.27	2.48
Discounting factor	$t = (l+r)^{i}$	1.05	1.10	1.16	1.22	1.28	1.34	1.41	1.48	1.48
Discounted cash flow (DCF)	$u = s/t$	(9.52)	(2.59)	2.76	3.06	2.63	1.82	0.64	0.32	0.82
Net present value	$U = \Sigma u$	(9.52)	(12.11)	(9.35)	(6.29)	(3.66)	(1.84)	(1.20)	(0.88)	(0.06)
Accumulated investments	$Q = \Sigma q$									
Accumulated depreciations	$D = \Sigma d$									
Invested capital	$v = Q-D$									
ROI	$w = g/v$									

r = discount rate
i = year number

Note: Capital symbols identify accumulated values. Negative amounts are in parenthesis. It is assumed that the corporation tax rate is 50% i.e. $f = 0.5e$

ANNEXE 3: FLIPSON LTD

The British electronics firm Flipson Ltd of Henley-on-Thames, Oxfordshire, recently developed a new type of hi-fi equipment, the so-called compact-deck. This is a combination of the compact disc player and a metal cassette deck, a very powerful piece of equipment which enables listeners to enjoy all the benefits of digitized sound. In addition, it is cheaper than the combination of compact disc player and high-quality cassette deck, because a very intelligent use has been made of integrated functions. The device can be considered an excellent piece of craftmanship that will have a great impact on the development of the audio market.

The project is out of the research laboratory but still requires some further development work. Earlier research costs were £375,000 in 1984 and £250,000 in 1985. From 1986 up to and including 1989 the project will require a back-up from the R&D department costing £250,000 per annum. The earlier R&D expenses must be taken into account when estimating financial return.

In addition to development activities, about £500,000 will have to be spent on design and preparation for production. These activities will be carried out in 1986; the corresponding expenses will be turned into assets.

Production and sales are scheduled to start in 1987. This requires an investment in equipment and buildings of £3.25m in 1986. Sales in 1987 should be 10,000 compact-decks, at a selling price of £250. This price will decrease annually by £25 until a level of £150 is reached in 1991. This is the very lowest price, in view of the continuing production costs of £125.

It is anticipated that the public will react enthusiastically, and partly because of these price reductions. Sales are expected to rise to 20,000 units in 1988 and 50,000 units in 1989.

After that, the full capacity of the plant – 100,000 units per year – can be sold.

As demand will still be increasing, a second plant is planned for construction in 1989; this will cost £6.25m for a capacity of 200,000 units. The plant will produce 50,000 units in 1990, then 100,000 units in 1991, 150,000 in 1992 and 200,000 units henceforth. By debottlenecking both plants in 1992 (costs: £8.75m) their capacity can be increased by 50 per cent. This extra capacity can be fully utilized as from 1993 onwards.

An operation like this requires a working capital of 25 per cent of sales. The cut-off rate for the internal rate of return is set at 13 per cent. The discount rate for the estimation of the net present value is to be set at 10 per cent. All investments will be depreciated in five years.

The discounted pay-back period, net present value and internal rate of return are to be calculated and commented upon.

Financial return analysis

Take 1986 as year 1. Results are given in Table A3.3.

(a) *Research costs*
These are $375{,}000 \times 1.10^2 + 250{,}000 \times 1.10 + 250{,}000 =$ £979,000 in 1986, and £250,000 for the years 1987, 1988 and 1989. Likelihood of success: 100 per cent.

(b) *Investments and depreciation*; see Table A3.1

(c) *Sales and costs*; see Table A3.2

From Table A3.3 the project appears to be very unattractive. The undiscounted accumulated cash flow only becomes postitive at the end of 1995 and the net present value at 10 per cent is very negative. The internal rate of return is about 2 per cent. This is much too low.

From these data we may not conclude, however, that the project is unattractive. A closer look shows that the cash flow *h* develops nicely, but the extra investments required in the years 1989 and 1992 cause cash flows *s* to be negative in

Table A3.1 Investments and depreciation (in £000s)

		Depreciation								
Investment	Year	1987	1988	1989	1990	1991	1992	1993	1994	1995
500	1986	100	100	100	100	100				
3,250	1986	650	650	650	650	650				
6,250	1989				1,250	1,250	1,250	1,250	1,250	
8,750	1992							1,750	1,750	1,750
Total		750	750	750	2,000	2,000	1,250	3,000	3,000	1,750

Table A3.2 Sales and costs

	Plant 1	Plant 2	Total	Price	Sales	Cost
1987	10,000		10	250	2,500	1,250
1988	20,000		20	225	4,500	2,500
1989	50,000		50	200	10,000	6,250
1990	100,000	50,000	150	175	26,250	18,750
1991	100,000	100,000	200	150	30,000	25,000
1992	100,000	150,000	250	150	37,500	31,250
1993	150,000	300,000	450	150	67,500	56,250
1994	150,000	300,000	450	150	67,500	56,250
1995	150,000	300,000	450	150	67,500	56,250

those years. In addition, there is a heavy demand for extra working capital all the time. The investments of 1989 and especially 1992 heavily depress the results, while the benefits cannot yet be taken into account, because of the limited horizon of ten years.

As there is much speculation about the effects of these investments and a decision on them is not required at this instant, it would be advisable to make an estimate of the first stage of the project only. This had been carried out in Table A3.4, which is identical to Table A3.3 except that the sales are now 17,500 for 1990 and 15,000 afterwards, costs are fixed at 12,500 from 1990 onwards, and the investments of 1989 and 1992 and their corresponding depreciations have been left out.

From Table A3.4 the first stage of the project comes out very well. The non-discounted pay-back period is four years and eight months after the start of production, which is not a very long time, but adequate if one takes into account that large R&D expenses have been accommodated which correspond in fact to a much larger project. In the calculation we have taken the conservative line that the first stage of the project should accommodate the integral research and development costs. In Table A3.4 the discounted pay-back period has not been computed. Instead, the calculation for the internal rate of return of 18 per cent had been given. This 18 per cent is a very adequate figure.

Table A3.3 Initial calculation for Flipson Ltd (in £000s)

Quantity	Code	Year									
		1986	1987	1988	1989	1990	1991	1992	1993	1994	1995
Gross sales	a	–	2,500	4,500	10,000	26,250	30,000	37,500	67,500	67,500	67,500
Research costs	b										
Likelihood of success	c										
Fictional research costs	$b_1 = b/c$	980	250	250	250						
Operational costs	b_2		1,250	2,500	6,250	18,750	25,000	31,250	56,250	56,250	56,250
Depreciation	$d = 0.2\,(n+o)$	–	750	750	750	2,000	2,000	1,250	3,000	3,000	1,750
Income before tax	$e = a-b_1-b_2-d$	(980)	250	1,000	2,750	5,500	3,000	5,000	8,250	8,250	9,500
Tax	$f = 0.5e$	(490)	125	500	1,375	2,750	1,500	2,500	4,125	4,125	4,750
ROI-income	$g = e-f$	(490)	125	500	1,375	2,750	1,500	2,500	4,125	4,125	4,750
Cash flow	$h = g+d$	(490)	875	1,250	2,125	4,750	3,500	3,750	7,125	7,125	6,500
Research investment	k										
Likelihood of success	m										
Fictional research investment	$n = k/m$	500									
Investment fixed assets	o	3,250			6,250			8,750			

Expansion working capital	p	–	625	500	1,375	4,063	938	1,875	7,500		
Investments	$q = n+o+p$	3,750	625	500	7,625	4,063	938	10,625	7,500		
Cash-flow – investments	$s = h-q$	(4,240)	250	750	(5,500)	687	2,562	(6,875)	(375)	7,125	6,500
Same, accumulated	$S = \Sigma s$	(4,240)	(3,990)	(3,240)	(8,740)	(8,053)	(5,491)	(12,366)	(12,741)	(5,616)	884
Discounting factor	$t = (l+r)^i$	1.10	1.21	1.33	1.46	1.61	1.77	1.95	2.14	2.36	2.59
Discounted cash flow (DCF)	$u = s/t$	(3,855)	207	564	(3,767)	427	1,447	(3,526)	(175)	3,019	2,510
Net present value	$U = \Sigma u$	(3,855)	(3,648)	(3,084)	(6,851)	(6,424)	(4,977)	(8,503)	(8,678)	(5,659)	(3,149)
Accumulated investments	$Q = \Sigma q$										
Accumulated depreciations	$D = \Sigma d$										
Invested capital	$v = Q-D$										
ROI	$w = g/v$										

r = discount rate
i = year number

Note: Capital symbols express accumulated values. Negative numbers are in parentheses. It is assumed that the corporation tax rate is 50%.

Table A3.4 First stage for Flipson Ltd (in £000s)

Quantity	Code	Year									
		1986	1987	1988	1989	1990	1991	1992	1993	1994	1995
Gross sales	a	–	2,500	4,500	10,000	17,500	15,000	15,000	15,000	15,000	15,000
Research costs	b										
Likelihood of success	c										
Fictional research costs	$b_1 = b/c$	980	250	250	250						
Operational costs	b_2	–	1,250	2,500	6,250	12,500	12,500	12,500	12,500	12,500	12,500
Depreciation	$d = 0.2\ (n+o)$	–	750	750	750	750	750				
Income before tax	$e = a-b_1-b_2-d$	(980)	250	1,000	2,750	4,250	1,750				
Tax	$f = 0.5e$	(490)	125	500	1,375	2,125	875				
ROI-income	$g = e-f$	(490)	125	500	1,375	2,125	875				
Cash flow	$h = g+d$	(490)	875	1,250	2,125	2,875	1,625	1,250	1,250	1,250	1,250
Research investment	k										
Likelihood of success	m										
Fictional research investment	$n = k/m$	500									
Investment fixed assets	o	3,250									

Expansion working capital	p	–	625	500	1,375	1,875	(625)				
Investments	$q = n+o+p$	3,750	625	500	1,375	1,875	(625)				
Cash-flow – investments	$s = h-q$	(4,240)	250	750	750	1,000	2,250	1,250	1,250	1,250	1,250
Same, accumulated	$S = \Sigma s$	(4,240)	(3,990)	(3,240)	(2,490)	(1,490)	760	2,010	3,260	4,510	5,760
Discounting factor	$t = (l+r)^i$	1.18	1.39	1.64	1.94	2.29	2.70	3.19	3.76	4.44	5.23
Discounted cash flow (DCF)	$u = s/t$	(3,593)	180	457	387	437	833	392	332	282	239
Net present value	$U = \Sigma u$	(3,593)	(3,413)	(2,956)	(2,569)	(2,132)	(1,299)	(907)	(575)	(293)	(54)
Accumulated investments	$Q = \Sigma q$										
Accumulated depreciations	$D = \Sigma d$										
Invested capital	$v = Q-D$										
ROI	$w = g/v$										

r = discount rate
i = year number

Note: Capital symbols express accumulated values. Negative numbers are in parentheses. It is assumed that the corporation tax rate is 50%.

Table A3.5 Integral calculation for Flipson Ltd (in £000s)

Quantity	Code	Year						
		1996	1997	1998	1999	2000	2001	2002
Gross sales	a	67,500	67,500	67,500	67,500	67,500	67,500	67,500
Research costs	b							
Likelihood of success	c							
Fictional research costs	$b_1 = b/c$							
Operational costs	b_2	56,250	56,250	56,250	56,250	56,250	56,250	56,250
Depreciation	$d = 0.2\ (n+o)$	1,750	1,750					
Income before tax	$e = a - b_1 - b_2 - d$	9,500	9,500	11,250				
Tax	$f = 0.5e$	4,750	4,750	5,625				
ROI-income	$g = e - f$	4,750	4,750	5,625				
Cash flow	$h = g + d$	6,500	6,500	5,625	5,625	5,625	5,625	5,625
Research investment	k							
Likelihood of success	m							
Fictional research investment	$n = k/m$							
Investment fixed assets	o							

Expansion working capital	p							
Investments	$q = n+o+p$							
Cash-flow – investments	$s = h-q$	6,500	6,500	5,625	5,625	5,625	5,625	5,625
Same, accumulated	$S = \Sigma s$							
Discounting factor	$t = (l+r)^{i}$	2.85	3.14	3.45	3.80	4.18	4.59	5.05
Discounted cash flow (DCF)	$u = s/t$	2,281	2,070	1,630	1,480	1,346	1,225	1,114
Net present value	$U = \Sigma u$	(968)	1,102	2,732	4,212	5,558	6,783	7,897
Accumulated investments	$Q = \Sigma q$							
Accumulated depreciations	$D = \Sigma d$							
Invested capital	$v = Q-D$							
ROI	$w = g/v$							

r = discount rate
i = year number

Note: Capital symbols express accumulated values. Negative numbers are in parentheses. It is assumed that the corporation tax rate is 50%.

Strictly speaking, the analysis ends here, as the first stage only is up for an investment decision. However, one would like to know more about the entire project. To this end, separate calculations for the two expansion investments should be made for a ten-year period. These calculations have not been included here. For those who want to check it out, the 1989 investment has an internal rate of return of about 15 per cent and the final investment an IRR of 10 per cent. This indicates that this last investment is unattractive from a purely financial point of view.

A wrong approach to the investment would be to compute NPV and IRR for the entire project for an extended period of time, say up to 2002, ten years after the expansion investment of 1992. This would come down to an extension of Table A3.3, which has been carried out in Table A3.5. At 10 per cent discount rate, the NPV now becomes £7,897,000 which of course is very attractive. The IRR will most likely be higher than the cut-off rate of 13 per cent.

The calculation of Table A3.5 might lead to the erratic conclusion that the entire project is financially attractive. As we have seen from the isolated analysis, this is only so for the first two stages. Two lessons can therefore be learned from this case:

- Don't let expansion investments contaminate the results of a financial return analysis.
- If a compound decision on a staged project is not required, always make separate calculations for each stage. Even when the compound project is viable, certain stages may not be. If a decision on the integral project must be taken, i.e. when a positive decision about the first stage would automatically tie up the proceeding decisions, then of course an integral calculation is required. In that case, the time period considered should be extended, in order to allow the benefits of the last stages to be taken into account.

ANNEXE 4: FRANZ WINTERMANN

Franz Wintermann took over his father's photography shop in Zürich in 1937. He managed to get through the war and found that there was a growing market for good, cheap cameras after the war. These cameras were hard to come by, however, so Wintermann decided to make them himself. Business prospered; Wintermann worked hard and lived soberly, putting most of the profits back into his company. In the sixties, Wintermann produced a series of cameras and sold them under his own brand name of KIKI. He also sold other cameras in his shops. The cameras he produced all belonged to the cheap section of the market.

Sales started to decline in the late sixties, due to increasing competition from low-waged countries, especially South-East Asia. The strength of the Swiss franc did not help Wintermann much, and his competitors produced quality cameras at a much lower price. Wintermann was forced to react to the current situation and decided to enter the market with a new product, for which there was as yet no competition.

He set up brainstorming sessions with his staff and carried out a systematic strength/weakness analysis. This resulted in the idea of producing a camera with instant photographic material. The know-how for this product was already available within the company, although much work still had to be done.

Before starting production, Wintermann got a market research bureau to investigate the potential market and the effects of various pricing policies. The work of the bureau was supplemented with cost data from the Wintermann production plant. The results are presented in Table A4.1.

The investment required for the project was $100,000 in 1972 for new machines. R&D costs (not to be converted into

Table A4.1 Data on instant camera and film project

Year	Number of cameras sold	Camera price	Number of films sold	Film price	Sales in $000s	Costs per camera	Total camera costs in $000s	Costs per film	Total film costs in $000s	Total costs in $000s	Working capital required
1971											
1972											
1973	2,000	150	3,000	10	330	130	260	9	27	287	16.5
1974	2,200	150	8,000	10	410	130	286	9	72	358	20.5
1975	2,500	150	12,000	10	495	130	325	8	96	421	24.8
1976	2,900	135	18,000	10	571.5	130	377	8	144	521	28.6
1977	3,400	135	25,000	10	709	130	442	7	150	592	35.5
1978	4,000	130	40,000	10	920	125	500	7	280	780	46
1979	5,000	125	60,000	10	1,225	120	600	6	360	960	61
1980	6,000	125	75,000	10	1,500	120	720	6	450	1,170	75

assets) were $60,000 in 1971 (likelihood of success of 75 per cent) and $40,000 in 1972 (likelihood of success 90 per cent). The investment should be depreciated in five years; corporation tax is 50 per cent.

Exercise 1

Estimate the internal rate of return for the period 1971-80 and comment on the results.

Solution

The solution from the above data is straightforward; it is presented in Table A4.2. From this table it appears that the internal rate of return is 22 per cent, which is excellent by any standard. The non-discounted pay-back period is four years and eight months after the start of production, which is reasonable. Since the idea for the project originated from a strategic analysis, the project meets the strategic objectives. Since it can be sold through proprietary channels, produced in facilities already available, with the required know-how also available, the synergistic criterion is also met and the project deserves the green light.

Case continued

Wintermann made a similar analysis and came to a similar conclusion; the development work was started as planned. This work continued favourably and the development work for 1972 was commissioned. A request for patents was accepted mid-1972.

In October 1972 Mr Wintermann's personal secretary suddenly came into his office with some bad news. The Swiss Federal Government had just passed a new law on environmental protection, and since production of the film required the use of delicate chemicals, the company had to apply for a permit under the new law. The factory had already been constructed, the development work was nearly finished, but production could not start.

Wintermann thought he could handle the situation because

Table A4.2 Instant camera and film project (in $000s)

Quantity	Code	Year									
		1971	1972	1973	1974	1975	1976	1977	1978	1979	1980
Gross sales	a			330	410	495	571.5	709	920	1,225	1,500
Research costs	b	60	40								
Likelihood of success	c	0.75	0.9								
Fictional research costs	$b_1 = b/c$	80	44.4								
Operational costs	b_2			287	358	421	521	592	780	960	1,170
Depreciation	$d = 0.2\ (n+o)$			20	20	20	20	20			
Income before tax	$e = a-b_1-b_2-d$	(80)	(44.4)	23	32	54	30.5	97	140	265	330
Tax	$f = 0.5e$	(40)	(22.2)	11.5	16	27	15.2	48.5	70	132.5	165
ROI-income	$g = e-f$	(40)	(22.2)	11.5	16	27	15.3	48.5	70	132.5	165
Cash flow	$h = g+d$	(40)	(22.2)	31.5	36	47	35.3	68.5	70	132.5	165
Research investment	k										
Likelihood of success	m										
Fictional research investment	$n = k/m$										
Investment fixed assets	o		100								

Expansion working capital	p			16.5	4	4.3	3.8	6.9	10.5	15	14
Investments	$q = n+o+p$		100	16.5	4	4.3	3.8	6.9	10.5	15	14
Cash-flow - investments	$s = h-q$	(40)	(122.2)	15	32	42.7	31.5	61.6	59.5	117.5	151
Same, accumulated	$S = \Sigma s$	(40)	(162.2)	(147.2)	(115.2)	(72.5)	(41)	20.6	80.1	197.6	348.6
Discounting factor	$t = (l+r)^i$	1.22	1.49	1.82	2.22	2.70	3.30	4.02	4.91	5.99	7.30
Discounted cash flow (DCF)	$u = s/t$	(32.8)	(82)	8.2	14.4	15.8	9.5	15.3	12.1	19.6	20.7
Net present value	$U = \Sigma u$	(32.8)	(114.8)	(106.6)	(92.2)	(76.4)	(66.9)	(51.6)	(39.5)	(19.9)	(0.8)
Accumulated investments	$Q = \Sigma q$		100	116.5	120.5	124.8	128.6	135.5	146	161	175
Accumulated depreciations	$d = \Sigma d$			20	40	60	80	100			
Invested capital	$v = Q-D$		100	96.5	80.5	64.8	48.6	135.5	146	161	175
ROI	$w = g/v$ in %		22.2	11.9	19.8	41.6	31.5	35.8	47.9	82.3	94.3

r = discount rate
i = year number

Note: Capital symbols express accumulated values. Negative numbers are in parentheses. It is assumed that the corporation tax rate is 50%.

Table A4.3 Delayed Wintermann project (in $000s)

Quantity	Code	Year									
		1971	1972	1973	1974	1975	1976	1977	1978	1979	1980
Gross sales	a					330	410	495	571.5	709	920
Research costs	b	60	40								
Likelihood of success	c	0.75	0.9								
Fictional research costs	$b_1 = b/c$	80	44.4								
Operational costs	b_2					287	358	421	521	592	780
Depreciation	$d = 0.2\,(n+o)$			20	20	20	20	20			
Income before tax	$e = a-b_1-b_2-d$	(80)	(44.4)	(20)	(20)	23	32	54	50.5	117	140
Tax	$f = 0.5e$	(40)	(22.2)	(10)	(10)	11.5	16	27	25.2	58.5	70
ROI-income	$g = e-f$	(40)	(22.2)	(10)	(10)	11.5	16	27	25.3	58.5	70
Cash flow	$h = g+d$	(40)	(22.2)	10	10	31.5	36	47	25.3	58.5	70
Research investment	k										
Likelihood of success	m										
Fictional research investment	$n = k/m$										
Investment fixed assets	o		100								

Expansion working capital	p					16.5	4	4.3	3.8	6.9	10.5
Investments	$q = n+o+p$		100			16.5	4	4.3	3.8	6.9	10.5
Cash-flow - investments	$s = h-q$	(40)	(122.2)	10	10	15	32	42.7	21.5	51.6	59.5
Same, accumulated	$S = \Sigma s$	(40)	(162.2)	(152.2)	(142.2)	(127.2)	(95.2)	(52.5)	(31)	20.6	80.1
Discounting factor	$t = (l+r)^i$	1.07	1.14	1.23	1.31	1.40	1.50	1.61	1.72	1.84	1.97
Discounted cash flow (DCF)	$u = s/t$	(37.4)	107.2	8.1	7.6	10.7	21.3	26.5	12.9	28	30.2
Net present value	$U = \Sigma u$	(37.4)	(144.5)	(136.4)	(128.8)	(118.1)	(96.8)	(70.3)	(57.8)	(29.8)	0.4
Accumulated investments	$Q = \Sigma q$		100			116.5	120.5	124.8	128.6	135.5	146
Accumulated depreciations	$d = \Sigma d$			20	40	60	80	100			
Invested capital	$v = Q-D$		100	(20)	(40)	56.5	40.5	24.8	128.6	135.5	146
ROI	$w = g/v$ in %					20.3	39.5	108	14.1	43.1	47.9

r = discount rate
i = year number

Note: Capital symbols express accumulated values. Negative numbers are in parentheses. It is assumed that the corporation tax rate is 50%.

he knew the city magistrates well and he had a reputation for being an honest and enterprising citizen. He underestimated the situation, however. The new law was not very clear in certain respects, and the Club of Rome's famous report on the Limits to Growth, published at the end of 1971, had turned the environmental issue into a politically highly sensitive one. All kinds of action groups started to interfere and Wintermann had to appear several times in public hearings. He was very disappointed and sometimes depressed about the situation, but there was little he could do. Only after two years did he get a permit to start production, on 1 January 1974. Unfortunately, the 1971 patent could not be extended, which could invite competition. In addition, competitors in the classic camera field had significantly improved their products, by adding electronic components and improved lenses, so the situation was much less attractive than in 1970 when the first financial analysis was made.

Exercise 2

Repeat the financial analysis for the 1971-80 period and comment on the results. Maintain sales and cost estimates.

Solution

The calculation is presented in Table A4.3. This table shows that the internal rate of return has dropped to 7 per cent.

Case continued

Wintermann's own analysts tell him he should abandon the project in view of the bad financial forecast, the stronger competition and the uncertainties about future environmental legislation. Wintermann, however, does not agree since he thinks that a full ten-year period should be taken into account. He calls in the market research bureau, which comes to the conclusion that the original sales figures should be shifted two years. The original 1979 and 1980 figures are no longer valid; lower figures will have to be used. These figures and the 1983-84 figures are presented in Table A4.4.

Table A4.4 Extended data on instant camera and film project

Year	Number of cameras sold	Camera price	Number of films sold	Film price	Sales in $000s	Costs per camera	Total camera costs in $000s	Costs per film	Total film costs in $000s	Total costs in $000s
1981	3,000	125	40,000	9	735	120	360	6	240	600
1982	2,500	120	35,000	8	580	120	300	6	210	510
1983	2,000	120	35,000	8	520	115	230	6	210	440
1984	1,500	115	30,000	7	382.5	115	172.5	6	180	352.5

Table A4.5 Revised Wintermann project (in $000s)

Quantity	Code	Year									
		1975	1976	1977	1978	1979	1980	1981	1982	1983	1984
Gross sales	a	330	410	495	571.5	709	920	735	580	520	382.5
Research costs	b	140									
Likelihood of success	c	1									
Fictional research costs	$b_1 = b/c$	140									
Operational costs	b_2	287	358	421	521	592	780	600	510	440	352.5
Depreciation	$d = 0.2\,(n+o)$		26.6	26.6	26.6	26.6	26.6				
Income before tax	$e = a - b_1 - b_2 - d$	(97)	25.4	47.4	23.9	90.4	113.4	135	70	80	30
Tax	$f = 0.5e$	(48.5)	12.7	23.7	12	45.2	56.7	67.5	35	40	15
ROI-income	$g = e - f$	(48.5)	12.7	23.7	12	45.2	56.7	67.5	35	40	15
Cash flow	$h = g + d$	(48.5)	39.3	50.3	38.6	71.8	83.3	67.5	35	40	15
Research investment	k										
Likelihood of success	m										
Fictional research investment	$n = k/m$										
Investment fixed assets	o	133									

Expansion working capital	p	16.5	4	4.3	3.8	6.9	10.5	(9.3)	(7.7)	(3)	(6.9)
Investments	$q = n+o+p$	149.5	4	4.3	3.8	6.9	10.5	(9.3)	(7.7)	(3)	(6.9)
Cash-flow investments	$s = h-q$	(198)	35.3	46	34.8	64.9	72.8	76.8	42.7	43	21.9
Same, accumulated	$S = \Sigma s$	(198)	(162.7)	(116.7)	(81.9)	(17.0)	55.8	132.6	175.3	179.6	201.5
Discounting factor	$t = (l+r)^i$	1.19	1.42	1.69	2.01	2.39	2.84	3.38	4.02	4.79	5.69
Discounted cash flow (DCF)	$u = s/t$	(166.4)	24.9	27.2	17.3	27.2	25.6	22.7	10.6	9	3.8
Net present value	$U = \Sigma u$	(166.4)	(141.5)	(114.3)	(97)	(69.8)	(44.2)	(21.5)	(10.9)	(1.9)	(1.9)
Accumulated investments	$Q = \Sigma q$	149.5	153.5	157.8	161.6	168.5	179	169.7	162	159	152.1
Accumulated depreciations	$d = \Sigma d$		26.6	53.2	79.8	106.4	133				
Invested capital	$v = Q-D$	149.5	126.9	104.6	81.8	62.1	46	169.7	162	159	152.1
ROI	$w = g/v$ in %		10	22.6	14.7	72.8	123	39.7	21.6	25.2	9.9

r = discount rate
i = year number

Note: Capital symbols express accumulated values. Negative numbers are in parentheses. It is assumed that the corporation tax rate is 50%.

Exercise 3

Estimate the internal return again and comment on other aspects. Should the project be continued, or not?

Suggested solution

The financial return analysis for the 1975-84 period shows an internal rate of return of 19 per cent with a non-discounted pay-back period of five years and three months after the start of commercial operations (Table A4.5). This is based on the new market expectations and the present 1975 value of research costs and fixed assets. The result is adequate but the commercial and environmental risks remain.

This calls for a real entrepreneurial decision. The answer is perhaps that the camera and film industry is moving towards the mature phase of the product life cycle. It is known that in the second half of this phase there is often a shake-out process in which small suppliers die while only a few larger ones remain to form an oligopolistic market. Franz Wintermann certainly does not have the power to become one of the large ones. He should therefore realize that if he goes on with the project he will not stay in business long. In such a situation the pay-back period becomes the important financial criterion, and this is not particularly good at more than five years. Will Wintermann have this length of time? Will he be able to sell the enterprise and know-how to one of the potential survivors? And what are the social costs of closing down the business if he fails to sell in time? Our guess would be that unless Wintermann has a solid interest from one of the larger companies in his enterprise he should abandon the project. Astute readers, however, might argue that he cannot sell something which is not there, and that he should take the risk and find a market niche if he fails to sell the firm. Ultimately, investment is an entrepreneurial decision and in cases like this, systematic analysis can clarify the situation, but it cannot supply the solution.

ANNEXE 5: FINANCIAL RETURN AFTER FINANCING

Introduction

The estimate of the financial return of an investment proposition, as described in Chapter 2 and the foregoing annexes, concerns the attractiveness of a project prior to financing. It implies that the effects of economic leverage due to partial external financing are not included. This corresponds to a situation in which the investor does not use debt financing but supplies all the funds required himself. We know that such situations are rare. In fact, virtually all enterprises use some kind of debt financing, if only to cover their working capital.

This raises the question as to which financial returns can be expected from the money the investor actually puts in himself. One can extend this question by requiring an estimate of the development of the profit and loss account and the balance sheet of the project as well as the development of a number of key financial ratios, such as the equity/debt ratio, the interest coverage, the return on equity, and so on.

It is relatively straightforward to modify the calculation scheme of Chapter 2 and to add a few tables in order to be able to calculate the financial return after financing and a set of financial ratios.

The forms

Such calculations can be performed with Tables A5.1-A5.7. We will first explain the use of these tables and then proceed to list the steps to be taken in the financial analysis. The tables in this annexe use the same symbols as Table 2.6; new quantities will be designated by double-figure symbols. Accumulated quantities are again designated by capital

Table A5.1 Profit and Loss Account

Quantity	Code	Year									
		1	2	3	4	5	6	7	8	9	10
Gross sales	a										
Research costs	b										
Likelihood of success	c										
Fictional R&D costs	$b_1 = b/c$										
Other costs	b_2										
Depreciation	d										
Income before tax and interest	$e = a - b_1 - b_2 - d$										
Tax (without interest effect)	$f = ct \times e$										
ROI-income (income after tax, before interest)	$g = e - f$										
Interest paid	ip										
Tax recovery	$tr = ct \times ip$										
Interest after tax	$it = ip - tr$										
Net income	$ni = g - it$										

symbols; the symbol *L* after a quantity refers to its value last year.

First, Table 2.6 is split into the profit and loss (P&L) account, the Finance Plan and the Financial Return Analysis (Tables A5.1, A5.2 and A5.3). The P&L account is identical to the first section of the original scheme, except for a section on interest. This section comprises the interest paid (*ip*), tax recovery (*tr*) and interest paid including tax effect (interest after tax, *it*). In this, $it = ip - tr$. The tax recovery *tr* is a function of *ip*. If the corporate tax rate is *ct* per cent, then $tr = ct \times ip$. Suppose that $ct = 40$ per cent, then the company in fact gets back 40 per cent of the interest paid from the corporate tax. Subtracting the interest after tax (*it*) from the ROI-income gives the net income (*ni*). Note that we do not yet compute the cash flow *h* in the P&L account. Finally, note that the depreciations (line *d*) will now be computed from Table A5.4.

The Finance Plan (Table A5.2) starts with the establishment of the cash flow. The investment *q* can be calculated in exactly the same way as in the original table. Note that the symbol *WCL* stands for: working capital of last year; this quantity can be taken from line *WC* of the previous year. The symbols *WC* and *WCL* have been written in capitals because they represent accumulated quantities.

From the difference between cash flow *h* and investments *q* we still have to subtract the repayment of debts (*rd*). This gives the funds available (*fa*). In the earlier years *fa* is negative; *fa* then means: sum to be financed. This sum is either financed by sums paid for shares issued (*sc*) or by accepting debts (*db*). If, in later years, *fa* is positive, the excess money will become available as dividends or otherwise (line *dd*).

In Table A5.3 the financial criteria before and after financing can be computed. This includes the pay-back period (PBP), the discounted pay-back period (DPBP), the net present value (NPV) and the internal rate of return (IRR). The upper section of Table A5.3 computes these data for the pre-financing situation. It is identical to Table 2.6, except that an estimate of the scrap value of the project is added to the cash flow. This scrap value is the sum that becomes available when the project is terminated. We have assumed this to be equal

Table A5.2 Finance plan

Quantity	Code	Year									
		1	2	3	4	5	6	7	8	9	10
Net income	ni										
Depreciation	d										
Cash flow	$h = ni+d$										
Research investment	k										
Likelihood of success	m										
Fictional reserve investment	$n = k/m$										
Capital expenditures	o										
Working capital	WC										
Expansion working capital	$p = WC-WCL$										
Investments	$q = n+o+p$										
Difference	$h-q$										
Repayments of debts	rd										
Funds available or to be financed	$fa = h-q-rd$										
If $fa < 0$:											
expansion share capital	sc										
Expansion debts	db										
Sum = fa	$sc+db = -fa$										
If $fa > 0$:											
dividends	$dd = fa$										

Table A5.3 Financial return analysis

Quantity	Symbol	Year									
		1	2	3	4	5	6	7	8	9	10
cf–inv. before financing	$s = g+d-q$										
Same, accumulated	$S = \Sigma s$										
Working capital	WC										
Liquidation of fixed assets	10% of AA										
Non-discounted project value	$SS = S+WC+10\%$ of AA										
Discounting factor	$t = (l+r)^{i}$										
Discounted cash flow	$u = s/t$										
Same, accumulated	$U = \Sigma u$										
Discounted scrap value	$SV = (WC+10\%$ of $AA)/t$										
Net present value	$UU = U+SV$										
Share capital paid in	sc										
Dividends paid out	dd										
Cash flow after financing	$ca = dd-sc$										
Same, discounted	$ud = ca/t$										
Same, accumulated	$UD = \Sigma ud$										
Net present value after financing	$UA = UD+SV-DB/t$										

to the working capital *WC* and 10 per cent of the fixed assets *AA*. When these are added to the accumulated cash flow *S* (*s* and *S* are identical to the variables of Table 2.6), the total cash flow *SS* is obtained. When the cash flows are discounted, the discounted cash flow *u* can be computed, similar to Table 2.6. The same symbols have again been used. To the accumulated discounted cash flow *U* we have to add the discounted scrap value *SV* to obtain the total net present value.

Next, the financial return after financing is computed. Now the cash flow (*ca*) consists of the dividends or the (negative value) of the share capital paid. This can again be discounted (*ud*) and accumulated (*UD*), after which the discounted scrap value is added and the discounted debts are subtracted to obtain the net present value.

In order to facilitate the computations of depreciations and debt repayments Tables A5.4 and A5.5 can be used. Each new capital and research investment respecting each new loan can be entered in the first column, after which depreciations and repayments can be listed under the appropriate year numbers. We assume that all payments and/or receipts take place at the end of the book year. This implies a number of things:

- Cash flows have to be discounted for the year in which they occur.
- Depreciations of investments start in the year after which investment is paid for; in Table A5.4 the various depreciations in each year can be added up to yield the total depreciations *d* for that year, which figure can be entered in Table A5.2.
- Debt repayments also start in the year after which the debt has been acquired; adding up these repayments yields the total debt repayments *rd* to be used in Table A5.2. By adding all debts acquired up to and including that year, the total remaining debt *DB* is obtained for that year. This figure can be used in Table A5.3.
- Finally, the interest payments also start in the year after a debt has been acquired. If we assume, for the sake of simplicity, that all loans are obtained at the same interest rate, then the interest paid (*ip*) is a percentage of the total debt position *DB* of the previous year. This figure

Table A5.4 Depreciations

Capital or research investment (n,o)		To be depreciated in (number of) years	Depreciation in year									
Year	Amount		1	2	3	4	5	6	7	8	9	10
Total depreciation (line *d*) in each year (sum):												

Table A5.5 Debt repayments

Debt (db)		To be repaid in (number of) years	Repayments in year									
Year	Amount		1	2	3	4	5	6	7	8	9	10
Total debt repayment (line rd) in each year												
Total remaining debt $DB = DBL + db - rd$												
Interest paid $ip = ir \times DBL$												

(*ip*) can be entered in Table A5.1. Obviously, *ip* for year 1 equals zero as year 1 is the first year in which debts can be acquired.

To these five tables in the financial return analysis we have added the balance sheet (Table A5.6) and Table A5.7 for the calculation of financial ratios. The latter are required as an indication of the soundness of the financing scheme. In the balance sheet the fixed assets at 31 December (*AA*) are equal to those of last year (*AAL*; in year 1, $AAL = 0$), plus the capital and research investments, minus depreciations. When the working capital *WC* is added to the fixed assets, the invested capital is obtained.

On the passive side of the balance sheet we have share capital and retained earnings, together forming the equity. The share capital equals that of last year (*SCL*) plus the expansion of share capital (*sc*) from Table A5.2. Retained earnings equal the net income minus dividends paid out; the accumulated value *RT* has to be added to the share capital *SC* to obtain the equity *EQ*. If we add the debt to the equity (debts *DB* are equal to last year's debts *DBL*, plus the expansion of debts *db*, minus repayments *rd*) we once more obtain the invested capital. If no mistakes have been made in the calculation then the values for the invested capital on the active and on the passive side are equal.

Finally, in Table A5.7, a number of financial ratios have been listed, using standard definitions. It is beyond the scope of this book to discuss the significance and the interpretations of these ratios.

The break-even point is a relevant item which has not been included in Table A5.8. The reason for this is that in the P&L account no distinction has been made between variable cost and fixed costs. If one does make this distinction (i.e. for $b_1 + b_2$) and if the planned plant occupation is known (as a percentage of the full capacity), one can compute for each year the break-even point as a percentage of full capacity by:

$$\text{Break-even \%} = \frac{\text{fixed costs} + \text{depreciation } (d)}{\text{gross sales } (a) - \text{variable costs}} \times \text{\% plant occupation}$$

Table A5.6 Balance sheet (at 31 December)

Quantity	Symbol	Year									
		1	2	3	4	5	6	7	8	9	10
Fixed assets 1/1	AAL										
Research investments	n										
Capital expenditures	o										
Depreciations	d										
Fixed assets 31/12	$AA = AAL+n+o-d$										
Working capital	WC										
Invested capital	$IC = AA+WC$										
Share capital	$SC = SCL+sc$										
Retained earnings	$rt = ni-dd$										
Acc. retained earnings	$RT = RTL+rt$										
Equity	$EQ = SC+RT$										
Debts	$DB = DBL+db-rd$										
Invested capital	$IC = EQ+DB$										

Table A5.7 Financial ratios

Ratio	Symbol	Year									
		1	2	3	4	5	6	7	8	9	10
Equity/invested capital	*EQ/IC*										
Equity/debt	*EQ/DB*										
Interest coverage, i.e. ROI-income/interest	*g/ip*										
Dividend return %	100 × *dd/SC*										
Dividend as % of net income	100 × *dd/ni*										
ROI % (return on investment)	100 × *g/IC*										
ROE % (return on equity)	100 × *ni/EQ*										
ROS % (return on sales)	100 × *ni/a*										
Capital return	*a/IC*										
Working capital/sales	*WC/a*										

This formula can be derived as follows: the break-even situation occurs when the sales just compensate the fixed costs (including depreciation) and the variable costs. In formula:

x. sales price = x. variable costs per unit + fixed costs + d
in which x is the break-even production in units/year.

Now, the sales price per unit equals the planned gross sales a divided by the planned production in units/year. If we call the latter y, then:

$$\text{sales price} = \frac{a}{y}$$

Likewise:

$$\text{variable costs per unit} = \frac{\text{planned (total) variable costs}}{y}$$

Substituting this yields:

$$\frac{xa}{y} = \frac{x.\ \text{variable costs}}{y} + \text{fixed costs} + d$$

Rearranging this yields:

$$x = \frac{\text{fixed costs} + d}{a - \text{variable costs}} \quad y$$

Dividing by the plant capacity z in units/year yields:

$$\frac{x}{z} = \frac{\text{fixed costs} + d}{a - \text{variable costs}} \quad \frac{y}{z}$$

in which x/z equals the break-even point as a percentage of capacity and y/z equals the planned plant occupation, also as a percentage of capacity. This explains the forms; we shall now proceed to their usage.

Using the forms

Again, we will do so by filling the tables in steps.

Step 1

For the full ten years, estimate in Table A5.1 the:

gross sales (a);
research costs, etc. (b,c,b_1);
other costs (b_2).

In Table A5.2, estimate likewise:

the research investments, etc. (k,m,n);
the capital investment (o);
the working capital (WC) and the expansions of the working capital (p; for year 1, $WCL = 0$).

From these, the investments can be computed (line q in Table A5.2). The research and capital investments (n and o) must now be entered in Table A5.4.

Step 2

Now Table A5.4 must be completed, which means that the depreciation system will have to be chosen. In a calculation like this, commercial depreciations are used. Sometimes the fiscal depreciation system differs from this and corrections would have to be included in the forms, but for the sake of simplicity we have left this out. The sooner an investment is written off, the earlier one has the benefits of the corresponding tax compensations, assuming of course that the initial losses of the project can be covered by the investor – for instance from profits from other investments – or that they can be fed forward to be matched with future profits; the latter of course is less attractive than the former.

For each investment, the year in which the investment is paid for, the amount of the investment, and the number of years of depreciation must be entered in Table A5.4. The depreciations can then be listed in the right-hand columns. Finally, the depreciations can be added up for each year to give the total depreciation d of that year. When Table A5.4 has been completed the depreciations d can be entered in:

line d of the P&L account (Table A5.1);
line d of the Finance Plan (Table A5.2);
line d of the assets side of the Balance Sheet (Table A5.6).

Step 3

The P&L account can now be completed up to and including line *g* for the entire ten years. The assets side of the balance sheet can now also be completed for the full ten years, yielding the invested capitals (*IC*) on the assets side.

Step 4

From now on we will have to proceed year by year. In the first year there are no debts to be repaid, as we have assumed that the repayment of debts starts in the year after which they have been acquired. For the same reason, $ip = 0$ in year 1. With this we can complete the P&L account and hence, with $rd = 0$, we can compute *fa* for year 1. This *fa* will be negative, so the question arises as to how to finance it.

This brings us to one of the most crucial decisions in setting up the financing of a project, that is the choice of the equity/debt ratio. This ratio refers to the relative amounts of equity and debt in the share capital.The lower this equity/debt ratio, the more use is made of the leverage effect of debt financing. At the same time, the vulnerability of the company is increased since, because of a possible rise in interest rates and/or fall in earnings, the leverage effect may become negative. However, the equity/debt ratio does not depend only on the risks the entrepreneur wishes to take as it is limited at the same time by what the banks are prepared to risk. Since bank policies differ in different countries and in different kinds of projects it is impossible here to quote general or desirable figures for the equity/debt ratio. For industrial companies in Great Britain and the Netherlands 40 per cent equity to 60 per cent debt is not an unusual figure to use in estimates for financial return.

Suppose we want a ratio of equity = debt of 40 : 60, then, using the symbols in Table A5.13:

$$\frac{EQ}{DB} = \frac{40}{60}$$

substituting the formulae for EQ and DB of Table A5.13:

$$\frac{SC + RT}{DBL + db - rd} = \frac{40}{60}$$

or:

$$\frac{SLC + sc + RTL + ni}{DBL + fa - sc - rd} = \frac{40}{60}$$

as $dd = 0$ when fa is negative, and $db = fa - sc$.

This formula can readily be solved for sc and hence rd.

For year 1, SCL, DBL, RTL and rd are 0 so:

$$\frac{sc + ni}{fa - sc} = \frac{40}{60}$$

Using the above formulae, sc and db can be computed, which completes forms A5.1 and A5.2 for that year.

Step 5

Next, Tables A5.5, A5.6 and A5.7 can be completed for that year. The debt expansion has to be carried to the table of debt repayments. In this table the year of the debt expansion can be entered, together with the debt expansion itself and the number of years in which the debt will have to be repaid. As we have assumed that debt repayment will start in the year following that of the debt expansion, the repayments in year 1 will be zero. After the debt expansions and the corresponding repayments have been filled in for a certain year, the total debt repayment rd for the next year can be found by adding up the repayments for the successive debts.

Next, the total remaining debt can be computed by adding debt expansions and subtracting repayments from the debts at the end of the previous year (DBL). For year 1, $DBL = 0$, and so is rd, so $DB = db$.

In the last line of Table A5.5, the interest paid ip for the next year can be computed as a percentage of DBL. This is based on the not so realistic assumption that interest payments only start in the year after which the debt has been acquired. As we shall point out later, this assumption saves us from a cumbersome iterative calculation for each year.

Next, the liability side of the balance sheet for the year just completed (Table A5.6) should be filled in. The *DB* of Table A5.6 can be taken from Table A5.5. The equity *EQ* can be readily computed and hence the invested capital *IC*. This *IC* must of course be identical to the *IC* of the asset side of the sheet. If it isn't, there has been a mistake somewhere.

Finally, the financial ratios in Table A5.7 can be computed for that year. This includes the equity/debt ratio which should work out at the value used in Step 4. If it differs from that, there has been a mistake somewhere.

Step 6

Now the calculation is repeated for the next year. From Step 5 we know the interest paid *ip* and the debt repayment *rd* for this next year. These figures can be entered into Tables A5.1 and A5.2 respectively, after which *fa* can be computed (repeat Step 3). If *fa* is negative, *sc* and *db* can be found by Step 4; if it is positive, *dd* = *fa* and the excess money can be paid out to the investor.

When *db* has been found (if *fa* is positive, then *db* = 0) it can be entered in Table A5.6, after which Tables A5.6, A5.7 and A5.8 can be completed for that year, following the description in Step 5. After this, the calculation for the next year can begin, until the calculations for all years have been completed.

Note that if *fa* is negative, share capital and debts will have to be expanded in such a way that the minimum equity/debt ratio is maintained. If, in later years, *fa* becomes positive, the excess money becomes available to the investor as dividends, if the investment is encompassed in a new company. If this is not the case, the money just becomes available as such. We have assumed that all the money generated after financing can be paid out as dividends or otherwise. Sometimes, however, there are legal restrictions to the amount of dividends that can be paid out; this is especially the case in developing countries. Furthermore, an investor can deliberately decide to leave money in the company, i.e. to limit the amount of

Table A5.8 Profit and Loss Account: example

Quantity	Code	Year									
		1	2	3	4	5	6	7	8	9	10
Gross sales	a	–	–	2,000	2,300	2,645	3,042	3,498	4,023	4,626	5,320
Research costs	b										
Likelihood of success	c										
Fictional R&D costs	$b_1 = b/c$	125	167								
Other costs	b_2	–	–	1,500	1,650	1,815	1,997	2,196	2,416	2,657	2,923
Depreciation	d	–	80	300	300	300	300	220			
Income before tax and interest	$e = a - b_1 - b_2 - d$	(125)	(247)	200	350	530	745	1,082	1,607	1,969	2,397
Tax (without interest effect)	$f = ct \times e$	(63)	(124)	100	175	265	373	541	804	985	1,199
ROI-income (income after tax, before interest)	$g = e - f$	(62)	(123)	100	175	265	372	541	803	984	1,198
Interest paid	ip	–	24	85	103	78	53	28	7	–	–
Tax recovery	$tr = ct \times ip$	–	12	42	51	39	26	14	3	–	–
Interest after tax	$it = ip - tr$	–	12	43	52	39	27	14	4	–	–
Net income	$ni = g - it$	(62)	(135)	57	123	226	345	527	799	984	1,198

dividends in favour of the building up of cash reserves. Multinational companies, engaged in joint ventures with local shareholders, will often do this, in order not to depend on the willingness of these shareholders to expand the company when the multinational so desires. We have left these options out because we are dealing with a financial judgement of the project and not with actual financing policy.

Step 7

Now that Tables A5.1 and A5.2 and A5.4 - A5.7 have been completed for the entire ten years, we can finally complete Table A5.3 and find the parameters by which the project is judged.

Table A5.3 consists of three sections, the first two of which correspond to the calculations included in Table 2.6, except for the addition of the scrap value. If one omits this scrap value, then $SS = S$ and $UU = U$, making the calculation of the net present value identical to that of Table A2.6.

The net present value after financing can be calculated in the lower section of Table A5.3. This calculation takes into account the money put in (*sc*) and received (*dd*) by the investor; these are in fact the investor's cash flows (*ca*). To the total discounted cash flow *UD*, one can add the discounted scrap value and subtract the discounted remaining debts in order to find the total value of the project for the investor.

Note

We have assumed that all payments and receipts occur at the end of the year. This implies, among other things, that the first interest to be paid for a loan comes in the year after the loan has been acquired. This is not entirely realistic, but it saves us a trial and error procedure, by which we have to estimate the interest first in order to be able to compute the net income *ni* and hence, in Table A5.2, the funds available or to be financed *fa*. From *fa*, a decision about the relative amounts of expansion share capital and expansion debts would have to be made. From the expansion of debts one could then compute the interest in the P&L account, and so on, until interest and expansion of debts correspond. For the sake of simplicity we have left this out. Similarly, we have assumed that all loans are obtained at the same interest rate. This is certainly not realistic, but for an assessment of the financial attractiveness of a project, these assumptions yield an accurate enough estimate.

Example

We will now compute the parameters before and after financing for the example in Chapter 2. The results are given in Tables A5.8 - A5.14, which correspond to the form of Tables A5.1 -A5.7. The steps correspond to the instructions in this annexe.

Step 1

The data a, b_1, b_2, n, o, WC, p can readily be copied from Table 2.8 into Tables A5.8 and A5.9 after which q can be computed. The investments can then be copied into Tables A5.11 and A5.12.

Step 2

Since it was decided in Chapter 2 to depreciate in five years, Table A5.11 can be readily completed. This yields the total depreciations d which can now be entered into Tables A5.8, A5.9 and A5.13.

Step 3

Table A5.8 can now be completed up to line g. The assets side of Table A5.13 can be completed.

Step 4, year 1

For year 1, ip = 0; this yields ni = (62) in Table A5.8. Entering this in Table A5.9, fa can be computed as rd_1 = 0. Let us now take the decision to finance by 40 per cent equity and

Table A5.9 Finance plan: example

Quantity	Code	Year									
		1	2	3	4	5	6	7	8	9	10
Net income	*ni*	(62)	(135)	57	123	226	345	527	799	984	1,198
Depreciation	*d*	–	80	300	300	300	300	220	–	–	–
Cash flow	*h* = *ni*+*d*	(62)	(55)	357	423	526	645	747	799	984	1,198
Research investment	*k*										
Likelihood of success	*m*										
Fictional reserve investment	*n* = *k*/*m*	–	500								
Capital expenditures	*o*	400	600								
Working capital	*WC*	–	–	600	690	794	913	1,049	1,207	1,388	1,596

Expansion working capital	$p = WC - WCL$	–	–	600	90	104	119	137	158	181	208
Investments	$q = n + o + p$	400	1,100	600	90	104	119	137	158	181	208
Difference	$h - q$	(462)	(1,155)	(243)	333	422	526	610	641	803	990
Repayment of debts	rd	–	48	180	252	252	252	204	72	–	–
Funds available or to be financed	$fa = h - q - rd$	(462)	(1,203)	(423)	81	170	274	406	569	803	990
If $fa < 0$:											
expansion share capital	sc	222	543	63							
Expansion debts	db	240	660	360							
Sum = fa	$sc + db = -fa$	462	1,203	423							
If $fa > 0$:											
dividends	$dd = fa$				84	170	274	406	569	803	990

60 per cent debt. In the formula from Step 4 for the first year, i.e.:

$$\frac{sc + ni}{fa - sc} = \frac{40}{60}$$

we can substitute for ni = (62) and fa = 462. The equation is then solved for sc = 222. This makes db = 462 – 222 = 240.

Step 5, year 1

The debt expansion of 240 for year 1 can now be entered in Table A5.12. In we take the decision to repay in five years and assume an interest rate of 10 per cent, then we can find rd_2 (which is 48), DB_1 (which is 240) and ip_2 which is 10 per cent of DB_1 = 24.

The liability side of the balance sheet can now be completed with SCL = 0, sc = 222, $rt = ni$ = (62), RTL = 0, and DB = 240. This makes IC = 400, which corresponds to the IC of the assets side.

Finally, Table A5.14 can be completed for year 1. Only the values for EQ/IC and EQ/DB make sense and they correspond exactly to the 40/60 ratio set earlier.

Step 4, year 2

With ip_2 = 24 and rd_2 = 48 we can find fa_2, which turns out to be (1,203). Using the formula:

$$\frac{SCL + sc + RTL + ni}{DBL + fa - sc - rd} = \frac{40}{60}$$

and substituting for known variables gives:

$$\frac{222 + sc - 62 - 135}{240 + 1203 - sc - 48} = \frac{40}{60}$$

which yields sc = 543 and db = 660.

Step 5, year 2

The debt expansion of 660 can be entered in Table A5.12 and depreciated in five years. This yields rd_3 = 180, DB_2

= 852 and ip_3 = 10 per cent of this = 85. Tables A5.13 and A5.14 can now be completed for year 2.

Step 6

For year 3, *fa* = (423). Using the formula yields:

$$\frac{756 + sc - 197 + 57}{852 + 423 - sc - 180} = \frac{40}{60}$$

which solves for *sc* = 63 and *db* = 360.

The latter value goes into Table A5.12 and this table and Tables A5.13 and A5.14 can be completed for year 3.

For year 4, *fa* becomes 81. This means that money can be paid out to the investor and that no debt expansion is necessary. As it can be readily seen that *fa* will remain positive for the following years, Table A5.12 can now be completed for all following years, and so can Tables A5.8 and A5.9, using the *ip* and *rd* values. The remaining debts *DB* should of course become zero in this example, with a short repayment time.

Finally, Tables A5.13 and A5.14 can be completed. The *IC*s on the liability side of the balance sheet correspond to those on the assets side, apart from round-off errors. In Table A5.14 the equity/debt ratio approaches infinity as debts approach zero; the equity/invested capital ratio likewise approaches 1. The ROI percentages are equal to those of Table 2.8, apart from round-off errors. The ratio of working capital to sales is 30 per cent, because we have so decided it.

Step 7

Now that all data have been obtained we can start the financial analysis of Table A5.10. In the first block *s* and *S* are readily computed, giving the same values as in Table 2.8. The undiscounted pay-back period, now computed from line *SS* (using *AA* values from Table A5.13) is five years and two months. This is shorter than the calculation in Table 2.8 as the scrap value has now been included.

Table A5.10 Financial return analysis: example

Quantity	Code	Year 1	2	3	4	5	6	7	8	9	10
cf–inv. before financing	$s = g+d-q$	(462)	(1,143)	(200)	385	461	553	624	645	803	990
Same, accumulated	$S = \Sigma s$	(462)	(1,605)	(1,805)	(1,420)	(959)	(408)	216	861	1,664	2,654
Working capital	WC	–	–	600	690	794	913	1,049	1,207	1,388	1,596
Liquidation of fixed assets	10% of AA	40	142	112	82	52	22	–	–	–	–
Non-discounted project value	$SS = S+WC+$ 10% of AA	(422)	(1,463)	(1,093)	(648)	(113)	527	1,265	2,068	3,052	4,250
Discounting factor	$t = (l+r)^i$	1.18	1.39	1.64	1.94	2.29	2.70	3.19	3.76	4.44	5.23
Discounted cash flow	$u = s/t$	(392)	(822)	(122)	198	201	205	196	172	181	189
Same, accumulated	$U = \Sigma u$	(392)	(1,214)	(1,336)	(1,138)	(937)	(732)	(536)	(364)	(183)	6
Discounted scrap value	$SV = (WC+10\%$ of AA/t	34	102	434	398	369	346	329	321	313	305
Net present value	$UU = U+SV$	(358)	(1,112)	(902)	(740)	(568)	(386)	(207)	(43)	130	311
Share capital paid in	sc	222	543	63	–	–	–	–	–	–	–
Dividends paid out	dd	–	–	–	81	170	274	406	569	803	990
Cash flow after financing	$ca = dd-sc$	(222)	(543)	(63)	81	170	274	406	569	803	990
Same, discounted	$ud = ca/t$	(188)	(391)	(38)	42	74	101	127	151	181	189
Same, accumulated	$UD = \Sigma\, ud$	(188)	(579)	(617)	(575)	(501)	(400)	(273)	(122)	59	248
Net present value after financing	$UA = UD+SV-DB/t$	(357)	(1,090)	(812)	(579)	(363)	(156)	33	199	372	553

Table A5.11 Table of depreciation: example

Capital or research investment (n,o)		To be depreciated in (number of) years	Depreciation in year									
Year	Amount		1	2	3	4	5	6	7	8	9	10
1	400	5	–	80	80	80	80	80				
2	1,100	5	–	–	220	220	220	220	220			
Total depreciation (line *d*) in each year (sum):				80	300	300	300	300	220			

Table A5.12 Table of debt repayments: example

Debt (db)		To be repaid in (number of) years	Repayments in year									
Year	Amount		1	2	3	4	5	6	7	8	9	10
1	240	5	–	48	48	48	48	48				
2	660	5	–	–	132	132	132	132	132			
3	360	5	–	–	–	72	72	72	72	72		
Total debt repayment (line *rd*) in each year			–	48	180	252	252	252	204	72	–	–
Total remaining debt $DB = DBL + db - rd$			240	852	1,032	780	528	276	72	–	–	–
Interest paid $ip = ir \times DBL$			–	24	85	103	78	53	28	7	–	–

Table A5.13 Balance sheet (at 31 December): example

Quantity	Symbol	Year									
		1	2	3	4	5	6	7	8	9	10
Fixed assets 1/1	*AAL*	–	400	1,420	1,120	820	520	220			
Research investments	*n*	–	500								
Capital expenditures	*o*	400	600								
Depreciations	*d*	–	80	300	300	300	300	220			
Fixed assets 31/12	*AA = AAL+n+o−d*	400	1,420	1,120	820	520	220	–	–	–	–
Working capital	*WC*	–	–	600	690	794	913	1,049	1,207	1,388	1,596
Invested capital	*IC = AA+WC*	400	1,420	1,720	1,510	1,314	1,133	1,049	1,207	1,388	1,596
Share capital	*SC = SCL + sc*	222	765	828	828	828	828	828	828	828	828
Retained earnings	*rt = ni−dd*	(62)	(135)	57	42	56	71	121	230	181	208
Acc. retained earnings	*RT = RTL + rt*	(62)	(197)	(140)	(98)	(42)	29	150	380	561	769
Equity	*EQ = SC + RT*	160	568	688	730	786	857	978	1,208	1,389	1,597
Debts	*DB = DBL + db −rd*	240	852	1,032	780	528	276	72	–	–	–
Invested capital	*IC = EQ + DB*	400	1,420	1,720	1,510	1,314	1,133	1,050	1,208	1,389	1,597

Table A5.14 Financial ratios: example

Ratio	Symbol	Year									
		1	2	3	4	5	6	7	8	9	10
Equity/invested capital	*EQ/IC*	0.40	0.40	0.40	0.48	0.60	0.76	0.93	1	1	1
Equity/debt	*EQ/DB*	0.67	0.67	0.67	0.94	1.49	3.11	14	–	–	–
Interest coverage, i.e. ROI-income/interest	*g/ip*				1.7	3.4	7.0	19	115	–	–
Dividend return %	100 × *dd/SC*				10	21	33	49	69	97	119
Dividend as % of net income	100 × *dd/ni*				66	75	80	77	71	82	83
ROI % (return on investment)	100 × *g/IC*			6	12	21	33	52	67	71	75
ROE % (return on equity)	100 × *ni/EQ*			8	17	29	40	54	66	71	75
ROS % (return on sales)	100 × *ni/a*			3	5	9	11	15	20	21	23
Capital return	*a/IC*			1.2	1.5	2.0	2.7	3.3	3.3	3.3	3.3
Working capital/sales	*WC/a*			0.3	0.3	0.3	0.3	0.3	0.3	0.3	0.3

Working out the second block for a discount rate of 18 per cent shows that the net present value becomes virtually zero. The internal rate of return therefore approximates to 18 per cent, identical to Table 2.8. If the discounted scrap value is added the net present value at 18 per cent increases from 6 to 311.

Finally, the net present value after financing at 18 per cent discount rate is 248 without scrap value and 553 including scrap value. The internal rate of return after financing turns out to be 25 per cent (giving a net present value of –3), which is considerably higher than the 18 per cent prior to financing. If the equity/debt ratio had remained 40/60, the internal rate of return after financing (let us call this *sc* on this occasion) could have been computed from the gearing ratio:

$$40 \cdot x\% + 60 \cdot 10\% = 100 \cdot 18\%$$

which solves for x = 30 per cent. The gearing effect is not fully utilized in this case because the debts have been repaid quite rapidly. It should be stated that in practice a company has short- and long-term debts, with an average repayment time of much longer than five years. In this case we have chosen five years to allow the debts to return to zero within the ten years considered for the analysis. This still shows the powerful effects of debt financing, as the internal rate of return on the investor's money increases from 18 to 25 per cent.

Reference Notes

1. H. Mintzberg, 'Planning on the left and managing on the right', *Harvard Business Review*, July-August 1976, pp. 49-58.
2. J. G. Wissema, 'Putting the technology assessment to work', *Research Management*, September 1981, pp. 11-17.
3. A good survey can be found in W. E. Souder, 'A system for using R&D project evaluation methods', *Research Management*, September 1987, pp. 29-37. Many of the methods described in this paper are very theoretical, however, and have little practical value. An alternative to the method of fictional R&D costs is one in which the cut-off rate is increased in cases of high technical or market risk. In practice this comes down to saying that one does not want to invest in risky projects as they rarely reach the increased cut-off rates. For this reason, and for the arbitrary way in which the cut-off rates are increased we prefer the method using fictional R&D costs and investments.
4. K. J. Mulder, 'Discounted cash flow analysis and investment policy', *Management International Review*, 1969, nr. 4-51, pp. 131-41.
5. J. R. Franks and H. H. Scholefield, in *Corporate Financial Management* , London, Gower Press, 1974, adequately cover the ways in which one can account for inflation in financial return analysis.
6. A clear discussion of this question can be found in Chapter 5 of Franks and Scholefield, op. cit . A somewhat more abstract, but elegantly written, discussion is provided by E. Solomon, *The Theory of Financial Management* , New York, Columbia University Press, 1963. However, most textbooks contain the same argumentation, so it does not really matter to which author one turns.
7. See note 5.
8. See note 6.
9. See Chapter 6 of Franks and Scholefield, op. cit. A classical paper on this issue is the one by D. B. Hertz, 'Risk analysis in capital investment', *Harvard Business Review*, September-October 1979, pp. 169-81.

10. Ibid.
11. This is described in J. G. Wissema, H. W. van der Pol and H. M. Messer, 'Strategic Management Archetypes', *Strategic Management Journal*, April 1980, pp. 37-47.
12. Ibid.
13. See, for instance, the excellent text by J. F. Abell, *Defining the Business, the Starting Point of Strategic Planning* , Englewood Cliffs, N. J., Prentice-Hall, 1980.
14. For some examples of the relation between functional policies and strategic planning, see J. G. Wissema, A. F. Brand and H. W. van der Pol. 'The incorporation of management development in strategic management', *Strategic Management Journal*, December 1981, pp. 361-77 and J. G. Wissema, *Strategic R&D Management* , to be published by Frances Pinter, 1986.
15. See note 4.

INDEX